John Oswald Mitchell

Burns and His Times

As Gathered from his Poems

John Oswald Mitchell

Burns and His Times
As Gathered from his Poems

ISBN/EAN: 9783744712705

Printed in Europe, USA, Canada, Australia, Japan

Cover: Foto ©Thomas Meinert / pixelio.de

More available books at **www.hansebooks.com**

BURNS AND HIS TIMES

PUBLISHED BY
JAMES MACLEHOSE AND SONS, GLASGOW
𝔓ublishers to the 𝔘niversity.

MACMILLAN AND CO., LTD., LONDON.
New York, - - *The Macmillan Co.*
London, - - - *Simpkin, Hamilton and Co.*
Cambridge, - - *Macmillan and Bowes.*
Edinburgh, - - *Douglas and Foulis.*

MDCCCXCVII.

Burns
and his Times

As gathered from his Poems

By

J. O. Mitchell, LL.D.

"Thy manners-painting strains"

Glasgow
James MacLehose and Sons
Publishers to the University
1897

GLASGOW: PRINTED AT THE UNIVERSITY PRESS
BY ROBERT MACLEHOSE AND CO.

CONTENTS.

	PAGE
PREFATORY, . .	1
I. THE LAND OF BURNS, . .	4
II. ASPECT OF THE COUNTRY, . .	14
III. FAUNA AND FLORA, .	18
IV. AGRICULTURE, .	23
V. LAND-HOLDING,	35
VI. HOUSES, .	39
VII. CLOTHING, ...	41

CONTENTS

	PAGE
VIII. Food,	47
IX. Drink,	54
X. Classes and Masses—	
The Landed Class,	64
The Middle Class,	68
The Working Class,	76
The Non-Working Class,	84
XI. The Church,	87
XII. Church Patronage,	98
XIII. Church Discipline,	101
XIV. Criminal Jurisprudence,	106
XV. Superstitions,	111
XVI. Politics,	113
XVII. Taxation,	115

CONTENTS

	PAGE
XVIII. CURRENCY,	117
XIX. PRICES, .	121
XX. RECREATIONS—	
Of the Gentry, . .	125
Of the Common Folk,	128

BURNS AND HIS TIMES.

TO-NIGHT[1] throughout Scotland, and outside of Scotland wherever a company of Scotchmen can be gathered, the memory of Burns will be drunk in solemn silence. The toast will be prefaced by the best speech that the company can furnish. The *motif* of the speeches will vary. Some speakers will analyze the poetry of Burns and his relations to other poets; the influences that went to the making of him, and the influences that have streamed out from him. Other speakers will dwell on his style, his mastery of rhythm and

---

[1] This volume has grown out of a paper that appeared in the *Glasgow Herald* of 25th January, Burns's Birthday, 1888.

of rhyme; what his native Scotch became in his hands—how clear, how terse, how graphic; what happy turns of thought dropped from him spontaneously, like the diamonds in the fairy tale from the princess's mouth, gems of expression, in cut and water equalling the best bequoted bits of Tennyson, and in their spontaneousness surpassing them as the bold lines of the fresco surpass the laboured structure of the mosaic. Other speakers, these the best worth hearing, will see in Burns's poems the most fascinating of autobiographies, and will set us up the portrait that Burns's own hands have painted, with the

> . . . *votum, timor, ira, voluptas,*
> *Gaudia, discursus,*

the tenderness and the wrath, the love and the lust, the bright hope and the settled gloom, the high resolves and the base self-indulgence, the good passions and the evil, that sweep by turns across his mobile features.

I have set myself a humbler task, needing

neither critical nor constructive power, but only some care in reading. I wish to see what can be gathered from incidental statements in his poems as to Burns's surroundings, the country he lived in and the people he lived among. What we gather may not be much, but it will be all wheat and not chaff; incidental statements by one who could not be mistaken in the facts are the best of evidence.

I.

THE LAND OF BURNS.

A LITTLE attention to the place-names will show that the land of Burns is not Ayrshire, but only a small part of it, a triangle roughly answering to the basin, or rather to the lower part of the basin, of the Ayr. This triangle has for its base the Bay of Ayr, from the "Cove" of Cullean on the south to the "well-fed Irwin" on the north, and has for its apex Mauchline Toun. The limits are well defined. Further to the south the Cumnock Hills are named, but they are the "distant Cumnock Hills!" Further to the north Galston Muirs are named, but they are the horizon over which "the rising sun . . . wi' glorious light is glintin'." Further to the east, in Muirkirk, lives his brother poet, Lapraik, and Burns must see him "tho' he should pawn his pleugh and graith"; but Muirkirk is altogether out of reach, and Lapraik must meet him half-way, "at Mauchline race or Mauchline fair." It was within this narrow territory that Burns (saving the visits to Edinburgh, the Borders, and the Highlands, and the later residence in Nithsdale) lived all his days; it was from it that he drew nearly every landscape, nearly every portrait, in his marvellous gallery; it was it that he set himself to sing into fame. It was as yet unsung. The thought angers him. He pledges himself it shall be so no more.

> "Ramsay and famous Fergusson
> Gied Forth an' Tay a lift aboon;
> Yarrow an' Tweed to mony a tune
>   O'er Scotland rings,
> While Irwin, Lugar, Ayr, and Doon
>   Naebody sings!

> "Th' Ilissus, Tiber, Thames, an' Seine
> Glide sweet in mony a tunefu' line;

> But, Willie, set your foot to mine,
> An' cock your crest;
> We'll gar our streams and burnies shine
> Up wi' the best!"

He has redeemed his pledge; for all time Irwin shall come down "with stately thud," and "Lugar's mossy fountains boil," Ayr shall still "kiss his pebbled shore," and "the rose and woodbine twine" on the banks and braes of Doon.

With never a place-name in it to guide us, we could still make a fair guess whereabouts on the map to look for the Land of Burns. It is on the sea—

> "The tide-swol'n Firth, with sullen-sounding roar,
> Thro' the still night dashed hoarse along the shore."

The "Firth" is the Firth of Clyde, for Ailsa Craig is a familiar object:

> "Meg was deaf as Ailsa Craig."

Sand stretches far inside high-water mark:

> "Low in a sandy valley spread
> An ancient burgh rears her head."

Further inland the country is hilly:

> "We'll sing auld Coila's plains and fells."

But the hills are not like the hills round Foyers, where

> "The eagle from his cliffy brow
> Marked his prey below";

they are not even like

> "Yon wild, mossy mountains, sae lofty an' wide,
> That nurse in their bosom the youth o' the Clyde";

they are neither too high nor too wild to be crossed, on a rough, dark night:

> "The westlin' wind blaws loud an' shill,
> The nicht's baith mirk and rainy, O!
> But I'll get my plaid, an' out I'll steal,
> An' owre the hill to Nannie, O!";

they are not steep and they are not rocky, for the streams they discharge wind down, and as they wind they score the face of the slope:

> "How lofty, sweet Afton, thy neighbouring hills,
> Far marked with the courses of clear-winding rills!".[1]

---

[1] The Afton actually flows into the Nith, not the Ayr, but the face of the hill is the same on either side of the watershed.

There are

> "Moors red-brown wi' heather-bells,"

and wide haughs where

> "the burns came down like waters
> An acre braid."

The streams have a special type. It is Bruar Water that Burns makes say:

> "Here, foaming down the shelving rocks,
>   In twisting strength I rin;
> There high my boiling torrent smokes,
>   Wild roaring o'er a linn";

his home streams uniformly run a smoother course:

> "The burnies wimple down their glens
>   Wi' toddlin' din";

> "Whiles o'er a linn the burnie plays,
>   As thro' the glen it wimpl't;
> Whiles round a rocky scaur it strays;
>   Whiles in a weel it dimpl't;
> Whiles glittered to the nichtly rays
>   Wi' bickerin' dancin' dazzle;
> Whiles cookit underneath the braes
>   Beneath the spreading hazel,
>   Unseen that nicht";

sometimes they move with even softer step, and

> "glide
> Like Logan to the simmer sun";

or like

> "Auld hermit Ayr steal thro' the woods."

So with their banks. In Aberfeldy glen

> "The braes ascend like lofty wa's,
> The foaming stream deep roaring fa's,"

but Auld Coila's banks and braes are slopes of earth dotted with bracken and broom, or thick with copse and wood, gentle slopes, where the bairns can safely run about and "pu' the gowans fine."

Some geological features of the district may further help us. Trap rock is evidently common:

> "I micht as weel hae tried a quarry
> O' hard whun rock";

softer stone there must be for the numberless dykes:

> "A cotter howkin' in a sheugh,
> Wi' dirty stanes biggin' a dyke,
> Barin' a quarry an' sic like";

lastly, we are on the coal-measures:

"Our laird gets in his rackit rents,
His coals, his kain, an' a' his stents."

These particulars singly do not amount to much, but I do not think they unite except in the basin of the Ayr.

It would be easier to identify the Burns country but for one strange gap in Burns's topography and in Burns's love of nature. The lines already quoted from the "Brigs of Ayr" and two lines in the "Vision" are all from which one would gather that the Land of Burns lay along the sea, and Burns's few other allusions to the sea show none of them any love of it.

From the gable of his father's cottage Burns could see the Bay of Ayr, sometimes even in our rough north sleeping in the sunshine, oftener crowded with the white-maned waves galloping before the west wind; on his left the Heads of Ayr rose from the water bluff and black; on his right the long green crescent ended with the cliffs of the Cumbrae and Garragh Heads; right in front of him Arran stood up in all its glory, and the morning light searched the glens and corries, and the Grey Mare's Tail danced and sparkled, and when the sun went down, peak and ridge stood out from the purple and gold. All this Burns saw as we see it now, but he gave it never a look of love nor a word of praise.[1] The trotting burn and the whistling robin, the primrose and the gowan, no beauty land-

---

[1] Burns, after all, is not so hard on the sea as old Burt is on the mountains. Here is the impression that the finest of our Highland scenery made on him:—
"There is not much variety in it, but gloomy spaces, different rocks, heath, and high and low. To cast one's eye from an eminence toward a group of the mountains, they appear still one above the other, fainter and fainter, according to the aërial prospective, and the whole of a dismal, gloomy brown drawing upon a dirty purple, and most of all disagreeable when the heath is in bloom. Those ridges of the mountains that appear next to the other—by their rugged, irregular lines, the heath and black rocks—are rendered extremely harsh to the eye by appearing close to that diaphanous body, without any medium to soften the opposition; and the clearer the day, the more rude and offensive they are to the sight."—*Burt's Letters* (Ed. 1822), I. 285.

wards was minute enough to escape him, but
he had no eye for that scenery which with
us most delights poet and painter. To him
the sea was a gloomy and fearful object:

"The tide-swol'n Firth with sullen-sounding roar";
    "the stormy wave
  Where mony a danger I must brave";
    "the doubling roar,
  Surging on the rocky shore";

it was a cold, cruel power, crushing its
victims or severing them from home and
friends :

 "Th' unwary sailor thus aghast,
  The whirlin' torrent viewin',
 'Mid circling horrors yields at last
  To overwhelming ruin";
 "Ye foam-crested billows, allow me to wail
 Ere ye toss me afar from my loved native shore";
 "But seas between us braid hae roared
  Sin' auld lang syne."

It is a curious but not an isolated fact. In
spite of our wonderful mixture of land and
sea, in spite of the Norse blood in our veins,
there seems to be something in us apathetic

to the sea. Scotch poetry smells not of the sea, but of the meadow, the copse, and the hill; we have had great land-fighters by the hundred, but have hardly added a name to the roll of naval heroes.[1]

---

[1] I can only remember these :—before the Union Sir Andrew Barton and Sir Andrew Wood, and after the Union Admiral Duncan and Lord Dundonald. I should perhaps add to the list Paul Jones, a scamp and a braggart, but a daring and able commander, a Solway man, son to the gardener at Arbigland.

II.

ASPECT OF THE COUNTRY.

WERE Burns to revisit "Auld Coila" he would find the great features of nature unchanged—the rising sun would still glint over Galston Muirs, and the rising moon glowr over Cumnock Hills, Logan would still glide to the summer sun, and hermit Ayr steal through his woods; but nearly everything else would be new and strange—the Kirktouns grown to villages, the villages grown to towns, the towns swollen out of kenning, and a new skin over the whole face of the country. Nowadays high farming has fenced, and drained, and snodded almost to the tops of the hills. In Burns's days there were hardly any enclosures. Animals at grass, unless one could

> "Ca' them out to park or hill,"

have to be tethered:

> "As Mailie and her lambs thegither
> Were ae day nibblin' on the tether";

so the Auld Farmer to his Auld Mare Maggie:

> "Wi' tentie care I'll flit thy tether
> To some hained rig";

the shepherd, when he leaves his charge,

> "... steeks his faulding slap";

the patch of grain on the Infield is protected by

> "... a corn-enclosing bauk";

and when the scanty crop is gathered in, the cows are left to wander freely over Infield and Outfield, bauk and all:

> "But if the beast and branks be spar'd
> Till kye be gaun without the herd,
> An' a' the vittel in the yard
>   Are theekit right,
> I mean your ingle-side to guard
>   Ae winter night."

What fences there weré were the sheughs and the dykes so often named, the sheughs (or ditches) being the only drains, and the dykes being either round the steadings or march-dykes. There are still moors in the district; but they do not bulk as they do in the Burns landscape, and the "whins," and the "brackens," and the "ragweed," and the "rash-bushes," and the "spritty knowes," and the "lang yellow broom" have fallen back before cleaner husbandry; even the "rough burr thistle"—the "symbol dear" spared of Burns's "weeder-clips"—has been ruthlessly ordered off the ground; the "meikle-stanes" have been broken up; and, if the "cresting-cairns" survive away up on the hill-tops, the near-home cairns, such as Tam o' Shanter passed or Leezie the wanton weedo, have disappeared before their natural enemy the dyke-builder. Fine turnpikes—not to speak of railroads—have replaced the Burns roads. These were very rudimentary. On their way to Mauchline, the "swankies young in braw braid-claith" have to keep "springing o'er the gutters"; Tam o' Shanter between Ayr and Kirk Alloway has to cross a ford; "the lang Scotch miles" take the unlucky traveller

"Through mosses, waters, slaps, and stiles";

and the Auld Farmer reminds his auld mare

"That day ye pranced wi' muckle pride
When ye bure hame my bonny bride";

the bonny bride, of course, riding behind her man on a pillion, and pillions coming of roads too bad for wheels.

III.

FAUNA AND FLORA.

EVEN these have changed. Burns gives us a long list of wild birds, nearly thirty of them. Of these the "whistling robin," the "mellow mavis," the "wailing cushat," the "wee songsters o' the wood," are still spared to us all, and the "springing moorcock," the "birring paitrick," the "lonely woodcock" are still left to the sportsman. But the "stately swan," the "rairing bittern," and the "grave sage hern" are scarce now-a-days in Kyle.

The times have very naturally been harder on the four-footed beasts than on the "commoners of air."

"The thummart, wil' cat, brock, an' tod"

are all practically extinct except the tod, and the tod has had his fangs filed. He is still a terror to the unprotected hen, but sheep are now pretty safe from him. When Burns wrote, the tod is the author of the "sheepcote spoiled," as well as the "blood-stained roost": Mailie's dying prayer for her lambs is that they may be saved

"Frae dogs, an' tods, an' butchers' knives";

and when the "Twa Herds" fall out, their flocks are asked,

"Wha noo will keep ye frae the fox,
  Or worrying tykes?"

Hares were more numerous in Burns's day than they have been in ours, even before the Ground Game Act. We might infer this from the existence of the great stretches of rough open Outfield, yielding just the cover and the long run that suit the hare; but we may also infer it from the way Burns speaks of her. He names her over and over again with all sorts of epithets and pet names—sure signs of familiarity. We have "wheeling hares," and "hirplin' hares," and "jinkin' hares," and "whuddin' mawkins," and "amorous pussies," etc., etc. On the other hand, Burns never names the rabbit; rabbits must have swarmed on the sandy dunes along the sea-shore, but Burns had no love of sea or sea-shore, and whene'er he took his walks abroad, turned his steps inland.

Burns did not care for "the flaunting flowers our gardens yield," but he had a passionate love of wild flowers, and he gives us a list of them almost as long as his list of wild birds. All of them—the gowan and the violet, the rose, "first of flowers," and the primrose, "firstlin' o' the year," the "little harebells" and the "stately foxglove," and the rest of them—are still there to delight the eye and scent the air, but, alas! the "primrose braes" and "lily leas" have mostly been grubbed up.

Grafting is named as a familiar art of the gardener:

> "As on the brier the budding rose
> Still richer breaks, and fairer grows."

Burns names very few forest trees, I think only the oak:

"On lofty aiks the cushats wail";

the ash, once:

"She stately like yon youthful ash";

and the pine, once:

"Gi'e me the cot below the pine."

This is just what we should expect. Ayrshire, which had once been covered with wood—*testibus* the "swirly auld moss aiks" still dug from every moss—had much less wood in Burns's days than in ours: the lairds had neither taste nor means to indulge in "barren timber." On the other hand, Burns so often and often speaks of copsewood trees, the "scented birk," the "milkwhite thorn," the "rustling holly" with its "polished leaves and berries red," as to show that much more natural copse and scrub was scattered about then than now, more "haz'ly shaws," and "briery dens," and "breathing woodbine bowers":

"Within the glen sae bushy, O,
Aboon the plain sae rashy, O."

One tree that is still extant will hardly be found in its old place. In the "Address to the Deil" we read:

> "When twilight did my grannie summon
> To say her prayers, douce, honest woman!
> Aft yont the dyke she's heard you bummin'
> Wi' eerie drone,
> Or, rustlin', through the boortries comin',
> Wi' heavy groan."

In those days the Devil was a perfect nuisance, always thrusting himself in where he was not wanted, and indulging in the frivolous and vexatious pranks of the fiend school-boy. The boortrie, it was fortunately discovered, was a valuable prophylactic, and it was constantly planted round the steading; there its shade was sometimes sought as a quiet retreat for the solitary musings and devotions of the old Covenanter folk. Now-a-days the enemy has given up his pranks for more serious tactics, old Covenanter folk and their old ways are passed away, and the boortrie is no more planted round the steading.

IV.

AGRICULTURE.

From the few allusions to other occupations we may infer that agriculture was the main occupation. The main products of the soil can be made out.

Wheat is grown in favoured spots:

"Let husky wheat the haughs adorn."

"The rustling corn" is oats, "corn" being applied (as elsewhere) to the grain most in vogue:

"An' shook baith mickle corn an' bear."

Bear, "the bearded bear," or barley is prominent; John Barleycorn was both eaten and very largely drunk.

Beans:

> "At e'en when beans their fragrance shed."

Pease, evidently field pease, which were a regular article of food:

> "To slink thro' slaps, an' reave an' steal
> At stacks o' pease or stocks o' kail."

Hay:

> "In simmer when the hay was mawn."

Clover:

> "While clover blooms white o'er the lea."

Lint (whose "darling blue" has been wiped out by cotton):

> "A twomond auld sin' lint was i' the bell."

There is a good deal of dairying. Butter often comes in, but always as an orra treat. For the Holy Fair, farls are

> ". . . bak'd wi' butter,
> Fu' crump that day";

at Hallowe'en

> ". . . butter'd so'ns wi' fragrant lunt
> Set a' their gabs a steerin'";

AGRICULTURE

and in days gone by, Nansie had

"... buttered his brose"

for the husband she now lichtlies to the very bairns.

If "the yellow treasure" is a rare luxury, cheese is common; even the cotter's wife has

"... her weel-hained kebbuck fell."

But it is only of skimmed milk after all:

"... sweet milk cheese, in monie a whang,"

is bracketed with the "farls bak'd wi' butter" as a special cate for Holy Fair.

Sheep are bred:

"The auld gudeman delights to view
  His sheep an' kye thrive bonny, O!"

and something has already been done to improve the breed:

"She was nae get o' moorland tips,
  Wi' tawtit ket an' hairy hips,
  For her forebears were brocht in ships
    Frae yont the Tweed:
  A bonnier fleece ne'er crossed the clips,
    Than Mailie's dead."

The pig is named:

> "An' wha was it but Grumphie
>   Asteer that nicht!"

but I see no allusion to bacon, and infer that the pig had to go to pay the rint.

There are repeated allusions to poultry. Even Poosie Nansie had a "chicken-cavie"; the "turkey-cock pride" had been seen and noted; and geese were pastured in the open land, as one may still see them in England wherever the common has not yet been enclosed:

> "Or faith! I fear that wi' the geese
>   I shortly boost to pasture."

The only vegetables named are potatoes:

> "Potatoe-bings are snuggit up frae skaith";

kail (or curly-greens):

> "An' hunger'd mawkin's ta'en her way
>   To kailyards green";

and onions:

> "As ane were peeling onions."

There is no notice even of turnips.

AGRICULTURE

Fruits are very rarely named—only the hardy but admirable gooseberry, once:

"As plump an' grey as ony groset!"

and of *fruits de luxe,*

"That sunny walls from Boreas screen,"

we have

"Peaches and cherries, with roses and lilies."

In "Hallowe'en" the apple wee Jennie "gat frae Uncle Johnie" was evidently a rare luxury, as likewise the "auld gude-wife's weel-hoarded nits."

On the other hand, bees are so often named that they have evidently formed a common part of the *petite culture.* They "hum round the gay rose," "hum round the breathing flower," "sip nectar from the openin' flower," and so forth; a tocher-hunter is told that

"It's a' for the hiney he'll cherish the bee";

and the witches rush at Tam o' Shanter,

"As bees bizz out wi' angry fyke,
When plundering herds assail their byke."

Honey must have been a sore temptation to the herd in days when the price of a pound of sugar would have made a big hole in his week's wage.

Farm work is carried on in a rude fashion. The plough has four horses:

> "My pleugh is now thy bairntime a',
> Four gallant beasts as e'er did draw";

and Burns himself at Mossgiel has

> ". . . four brutes o' gallant mettle
> As ever drew before a pettle."

So common was the four-in-hand that there are regular names for each of the team: see "The Inventory." The names of only three are actually given there: the "Lan' ahin" (or nigh wheeler), the "Lan' afore" (or nigh leader), and the "Fur ahin" (or off wheeler): the fourth, described as a "Highland Donald hastie," was the "Fur afore" (or off leader). The "Lan' ahin," otherwise the "Fittielan'," had the hardest work of the team. Hence the special force of the line in " The Auld Farmer's

Salutation of his Auld Mare":

> "Thou wast a noble *fittie-lan'*
> As e'er in tug or tow were drawn."

The four-some team was needed, not that the "brutes" were poor (Burns expects "fifteen pun at least" for his "cowt," and the Auld Farmer tells his auld mare that her progeny that he had

> ". . . sell't awa'
> . . . drew me thritteen pounds an' twa,
> The vera warst,"

good prices as money values went), but partly because of the rough unclean ground, the "muckle stanes" and "spritty knowes" and other obstacles to be overcome, partly because of the clumsy wooden plough. The wonder is what Ayrshire pith and muscle could do in all the circumstances. Hear the Auld Farmer once more:

> "Aft thee an' I, in aught hours gaun,
> On guid March weather,
> Hae turned sax rood beside our han'
> For days thegither."

Horses are not the only draught animals:

> "And owsen frae the furrowed field
> Return sae dowf an' weary O!"

> "And o'er the lea I look sae fain,
> When Jockie's owsen hameward ca'."

On a few north-country farms oxen (which had disappeared from Scotland unless as eatables) have been of late years re-introduced as draught animals: they must once have been quite common: we can tell this from an "Oxgate of land," and from Oxgang, Oxwell, Oxenam, Oxenford, and other place-names. Harrowing was perhaps left for lighter beasts:

> "An' pownies reek in pleugh or braik."

Traces are made either of raw hide or of rope, leather and chain being unknown:

> ". . . a worthy beast
> As e'er in tug or tow was traced,"

"tug" being a strip of raw hide. Tethers either were cord, or were home-made from the hair of the beasts' tails. Mailie's dying prayer for her lambs is

> "Oh bid him never tie them mair
> Wi' wicked strings o' hemp and hair."

Branks—

> "And then its shanks,
> They were as thin, as sharp an' sma'
> As cheeks o' branks"—

were an arrangement of wood and rope which did duty for a bridle. Brechan is the horse-collar:

> "Wi' braw new branks in meikle pride,
> And eke a braw new brechan."

The grain is, of course, cut with the hook:

> "Still shearing an' clearing
> The tither stookit raw";

and the squad of shearers have to keep time with the "stibble-rig."

The crop is by no means safe even when stacked. Backward husbandry means late harvests, and in a late harvest in Scotland "stuff" has a good chance to be "unco green." There is a provision for such a case: the stack is ventilated by the "fause hoose," which we hear of in "Hallowe'en." Thanks to the "fause hoose," or it may be to slovenly building, the stack sometimes threatens to capsize, and has to be "timmer-propt for thrawin'," as Will's "nieves" find to their cost.

Threshing is done with the flail, the "thresher's weary flinging tree." Thus with John Barleycorn,

> "They laid him down upon his back,
> An' cudgelled him full sair."

Threshing is reckoned light work:

> "When I was beardless, young, and blate,
> An' first could thresh the barn":

and of the "three mischievous boys" at Mossgiel one is "a thrasher." The winnowing machine was unknown, and when it was first introduced was violently opposed as an arrogating of a function of the Creator, a presumptuous *making* of "devil's wind," as they called it; the old way was to throw the grain up,

AGRICULTURE

and hand-fan the caff out of it. Thus John Barleycorn :

"They hung him up before the storm."

In the process they use a "wecht," a sort of magnified tambourine :

"Meg fain wad tae the barn gaen,
To win' three wechts o' naething."

This way of winnowing explains why, viz. for the sake of the cross draught, two doors facing each other are always found in old barns, and gives a fine meaning to a line not otherwise understandable :

"The wakened lavrock warbling springs,
An' climbs the early sky,
Winnowing blythe her dewy wings
In morning's rosy eye."

And the rudeness of all these appliances explains how on Mossgiel, a farm of 118 acres, Burns, besides his two brothers and himself and his mother and three sisters, needs three boys to help him :

"A gaudsman ane, a thrasher t'other,
Wee Davock hauds the nowt in fother."

The smaller implements, "the spades, the mattocks, and the hoes," "the shools an' knapping hammers," "the graip," etc., which are probably as old as Triptolemus, would be the same as our own, but clumsier. Only one of them needs notice. The wife of that unlucky wabster, Willie Wastle, among other charms, has "walie nieves like midden creels." The midden creel was essential; it carried out the manure to the Infield. It has now dropped out of use in the Lowlands, but it is still at work in the Highlands. On hundreds of crofts, any day in potato-planting, the crofter's wife may be seen, as Henry George saw her, peching along under the creel full of sea-ware for the "lazy beds," while the crofter, leaning by the door-cheek, moodily sucks his pipe and revolves his wrongs.

V.

LAND-HOLDING.

IN Kyle, as in Scotland generally, a good deal of the land used to be held by "bonnet lairds," farmers who, like English yeomen, owned their own farms, and who had their name because they wore the Scotch bonnet, and did not attempt the cocked hat of the gentry. To this class belong Tam Glen's rival, "Lowrie, the laird of Drumeller," who could not think more of himself if he were laird of Eglinton or Colean, and the "braw wooer" who is able to offer

"A weel stockit mailing, himsel' for the laird."

But for the most part the land carried "the

laird, the tenant, and the cotter." We hear something of all three. To begin with the laird:

> "Our laird gets in his rackit rents,
> His coals, his kain, an' a' his stents."

We have changed all this. An addition to the money rent has driven from the field the multures, the kain fowls, the driving of coals, and the other *droits de seigneur*. What is more to the purpose, we have opened fire on the "rackit rents." From Burns's day to our own, under the demoralizing influence of ownership, landlords have constantly exacted a competition price for the use of their land, and taken for the contingent produce the best offer they could get. How unlike the poor but honest cultivator, who would scorn to extort a competition price for the actual produce, or to cost his milk or his meal or his mutton without consulting the consumer! We have at last made a beginning of better things, and our brilliant success so far insures the spread of the new system. We cannot refuse to the rest of the Tetrarchy the blessings which have secured the gratitude and affection of our Celtic allies, nor limit to the hirer of land, principles that equally apply to the hirer of houses or the consumer of commodities. Soon, we may hope, competition-price shall be as extinct as Ship-money, and a man shall no more be held to a bad bargain than to a contract of personal servitude. Unluckily it was not so in Burns's time. The tenants were allowed to bid as much rent as ever they chose, and if they could not pay up at Whissenday and Martinmas, they had to "thole the factor's snash," and, may be, worse things. They were undeniably poor (the whole produce of their little farms, as farming then was, would not have made them rich):

> "Our whipper-in, wee blastit wonner,
> Poor worthless elf, it eats a dinner
> Better than ony tenant man
> His Honour has in a' the lan'";

and the cotters, with

> ". . . nocht but a cothouse and yaird,"

are even worse off:

> "An' what poor cot-folk pit their painch in,
> I own it's past my comprehension."

Our labourers live better than that. Yet the old cotter's bill of fare includes one luxury almost unknown to his successors:

> "The soupe their only Hawkie doth afford,
> That 'yont the hallan snugly chows her cud."

The cotter has the three acres and a cow! The three acres, such as they were, were not ill to get in those days of sparse population and rough, open land; but the cow represented marvellous self-denial, for the penny fee off which the cotter had saved her price after supporting "himsel', his wife, and smytrie o' wee duddy weans," was such as a hafflin of our day would scoff at.

VI.

HOUSES.

THESE were very bad. We are not surprised at Poosie Nansie's quarters:

> "He ended, an' the kebars sheuk
>   Aboon the loud uproar;
> The frichtit rattons backward leuk,
>   An' seek the benmost bore."

But Burns's own house is little better. It is entered by the rudest of door fastenings:

> "When click! the string the sneck did draw";

and by the loosest of doors:

> "While frosty winds blaw in the drift
>   Ben to the chimley lug,
> I grudge a wee the great folks' gift,
>   That leeve sae bien an' snug."

It certainly has a spence, but things are not much better there:

> "There, lanely, by the ingle cheek
> I sat and eyed the spewing reek
> That filled wi' host-provoking smeek
>   The auld clay biggin',
> An' heard the restless rattons squeak
>   Aboot the riggin'."

The "auld clay biggin'" was the farmhouse of Mossgiel, a farm of 118 acres and £90 rent. We may be sure that the labourer's "theekit cot" was much worse, yet it could be a home a prince might envy:

> "His wee bit ingle, blinkin' bonnily,
> His clean hearthstane, his thrifty wifie's smile,
> The lisping infant prattling on his knee,
> Does a' his weary carking cares beguile,
> An' makes him quite forget his labour an' his toil."

VII.

CLOTHING.

To begin at the top, Ayrshire is the home of the knitted and waulked bonnet. This admirable head-gear, whose merits have been in our day discovered by gentlemen, and even by ladies, is not at all worn now as it was. In Burns's day all countrymen of or under the rank of Bonnet Lairds wore the bonnet on all occasions. It stood their roughest work, and it was their best as well. Tam o' Shanter

> " . . . skelpit on thro' dub an' mire,
> Whiles haudin' fast his guid blue bonnet";

the auld guidman, to say grace in the change-house,

> " . . . aff his bonnet lays";

the elder at the plate wears it:

> "A greedy glow'r Black Bonnet throws,
> An' we maun draw our tippence";

even the minister has

> ". . . gown, an' ban', an' douce black bonnet";

they wear it at funerals, with the ghastly bobs in vogue on such occasions:

> "An' Robin's bonnet wave wi' crape";[1]

and the rural masher, when decked in all his bravery, still wears it. We have the complete masher outfit:

> "His coat is the hue of his bonnet sae blue,
> His fecket is white as the new driven snaw,
> His hose they are blae, and his shoon like the slae,
> An' his clear siller buckles they dazzle us a'."[2]

---

[1] Another emblem of woe was "weepers," bands of white muslin stitched over the coat cuffs at funerals:

> "Auld cantie Kyle may weepers wear,
> An' stain them wi' the saut, saut tear."

[2] A fecket is a sleeved waistcoat, like a groom's. Burns gives us his own masher outfit in "the Ronalds of the Bennals."

CLOTHING

No doubt the masher's coat, like the coats of the "swankies young" at the "Holy Fair," is of "braw braid claith," but the common wear is rough woollen home-spun:

> "What tho' on hamely fare we dine,
> Wear hodden grey and a' that."

The legs are sometimes encased in the same stuff, like

> "The vera grey breeks o' Tam Glen";

sometimes in blue plush (like our marvellous carters' waistcoats with the vast pearl buttons):

> "Thir breeks o' mine, my only pair,
> That ance were plush o' guid blue hair."

The "breeks" are veritable knee-breeches:

> "The lads sae trig, wi' wooer babs
> Weel knotted on their garten";

(with trousers these babs, the recognized signal of a purpose of proposal, would have been invisible.) "Hose" are of course long stockings. "Shoon" are repeatedly mentioned:

> "and stockings and pumps to put on my stumps."

The plaid is worn over all as a wrap:

> "I'll get my plaid, an' out I'll steal,
> An' owre the hills to Nannie O!"

but it is specially the mark of the shepherd:

> "Ye wha were ne'er by lairds respeckit
> To wear the plaid,
> But by the brutes themselves eleckit
> To be their guide."

Place aux dames. Except "Miss's fine Lunardi," the fashionable bonnet just named from the famous aeronaut, the only woman's head-dress given by Burns is the "auld wife's flannen toy": women as a rule had their heads bare, or covered them by a graceful fold of the plaid: the auld wife's "toy" was a close-fitting cap hanging down over the shoulders, like the linen covers of our soldiers' caps in the Tropics. The famous "Cutty Sark" is made of "Paisley harn," or coarse linen cloth. It costs 3s. 4d. ("twa pun Scots"), which I am told would be a high price now-a-days for a full size. What the price would have been for "snaw-white seventeen hundred linen" we are unfortunately not told. But both this fine fabric and the harn were orra articles; "flannen," which the witches had stuck to after "inlisting in the core," was the common wear. Jenny's "jimps and jirkinet," easy stays and shortgown, are contrasted with

> "My lady's gown with gairs upon't,
> And gowden flowers sae rare upon't."

In the "Vision" Coila wears a "robe of tartan sheen," and in the "Holy Fair" Fun, Superstition, and Hypocrisy wear "manteeles." How far these were in real use I cannot say, but one sketch is certainly from life. Women go to and from church barefoot, wearing the "shoon" only during the service:

> "The lasses, skelpin' barefit thrang,
> In silks an' scarlet glitter";

and

> "At slaps the billies bide a blink,
> Till lasses strip their shoon."

I can myself remember this good old act of thrift, now I fear given up. Country girls, "barefit carlins" whose best foot-gear for the six week days had been hoggars, tramped to church in their Sunday braws, carrying in one hand (besides sometimes a parasol) a white napkin folded round the Bible and the sprig of southernwood, and in the other hand a bundle containing the shoes and stockings; they stopped at the nearest burn to the church to wash their feet before putting on the shoes and stockings, and on the way home they stopped again to take these off. In church itself they were as scrupulous to be shod as if the Apostle's command to women had been to cover the feet instead of the head.

VIII.

FOOD.

First on the list stands

> "The hailsome parritch, chief o' Scotia's food."

This is served out in little wooden dishes:

> "An' I hae seen their cogie fou',
> That yet hae tarrow't at it;
> But or the day was done, I trow,
> The laggen they hae clautet."

It is sometimes eaten with milk:

> "The soupe their only Hawkie does afford";

and sometimes with beer:

> "Yet humbly kind in time o' need,
> The poor man's wine:
> His wee drap parritch and his bread
> Thou kitchens fine."

"Parritch," however, implied more cooking than was always available. There are two simpler preparations of the oatmeal:

(1) Crowdie, stir-about of oatmeal and hot water, with no subsequent boiling:[1]

"Then I gaed hame at crowdie time";

and,

(2) Drummock, stir-about of oatmeal and cold water, which does not sound appetizing:

"To tremble under Fortune's cummock,
An' scarce a bellyfu' o' drummock."

The oatmeal, which is boiled into parritch, is also baked into the "bread" mentioned above. There is no sign of ovens; the baking is on the ever-ready girdle:

"Wi' jumping an' thumping,
The vera girdle rang."

---

[1] Our invaluable friend Hawkie describes the making of crowdie, "and mixed with butter or kitchen fee it makes a strong food." In South Shields Hospital they dieted him on a "villainously weak decoction of oatmeal known as boilies."—*Hawkie's Autobiography*, 70. 111.

FOOD

On extra occasions the oatcake is enriched:

> "An' farls baked wi' butter,
> Fu' crump that day."

The meal used is sometimes "poke-meal." The numerous beggars who tramped from house to house got very little money. The regular dole was a handful of meal from the meal barrel beside the kitchen fire. This was dropped into the beggar's "poke," and there were regular merchants for the "poke-meal":

> "First, neist the fire, in auld red rags,
> Sat ane weel brac'd wi' mealy bags";

and again,

"When the t'other bag I sell, an' the t'other bottle tell";

and again,

"They toomed their pokes, and pawn'd their duds."[1]

---

[1] Hawkie speaks constantly of "poke-meal." It was measured by "tankards," apparently equal to pounds. Eight tankards made a "jigger's peck," and sold at Ecclefechan in 1815 for 3d. At Crieff (date not given) he pays his "tippence" for a night's lodging, with three tankards that he could put his arm into up to the elbow, and that must have held 3 lb.—*Hawkie's Autobiography*, 18, 60.

But oatmeal, though the commonest, is not the only grain eaten. We read of the "barley-miller," from whose "heapit happer" the material flowed for a softer bread than oatcake. Among the royal qualities of "John Barleycorn, the king of grain," we read:

> "On thee aft Scotland chows her cood
> In souple scones, the wale o' food."

So again,

> "Fortune, if thou'lt but gie me still
> Hale breeks, a scone, an' whisky gill";

and,

> "It's cryin' here for bakes and gills."

There is still another kind of bread:

> "Tell yon guid bluid o' auld Boconnock's
> I'll be his debt twa mashlum bannocks."

Mashlum bannocks, or scones, were made of a mixture of all sorts of meal, and very good they were, though the colour was against them; they were black from the mixture in them of meal from the field pease and beans.

The regular Hallowe'en supper is

"Butter'd sow'ns wi' fragrant lunt,"

sowans being a sort of soured *blanc mange* of grains of oats, very nasty even unbuttered.

I have spoken elsewhere of the use of butter and cheese, and of vegetables as far as these were known.

After the porridge and the oatcake the commonest article of food is Scotch broth or kail. This may occasionally contain meat. Thus John Barleycorn is described as

" . . . tumblin' in the boilin' flood
   Wi' kail or beef."

But the broth is oftener a *soupe maigre*:

"I'll sit down by my scanty meal,
Be't water brose or muslin kail,
   Wi' cheerfu' face,
As lang's the Muses dinna fail
   To say the grace."

The treasures of the sea seem to have been even less worked in Burns's day than in ours. The herring—which was then a staple article with Glasgow working folks—[1] is only named in what we may call proverbs:

"Ah, Tam! ah, Tam! thou'll get thy fairin'!
In hell they'll roast thee like a herrin'!"

and Dr. Hornbook threatens:

"I'll nail the self-conceited Sot
As dead's a herrin'."

The only other fish food named is in the elegy on Captain Mathew Henderson,

"An' like stock-fish come o'er his studdie
Wi' thy auld sides."

Butcher meat is expressly named as the diet of the gentles:

"Gi'e drippin' roasts to kintra lairds."

---

[1] Gibson, a contemporary of Burns, says that the Glasgow mechanics (average wage, 7s. a week) largely lived on herrings and potatoes, off which they could have an ample dinner for 1½d., and "no set of people in the world is healthier." Apoplexy, so common in England, "is scarce known here" (small blame to it). Gibson's *History of Glasgow in* 1777, p. 201.

FOOD

Burns's friends are little beholden to the butcher except for

> "Painch, tripe, or thairm,"

and for ingredients for the haggis. Moorlan' herds, however, have a chance of

> "Guid fat braxies."

Braxy mutton is a delicacy not to be found on our *menus*, and I have no knowledge of its merits, but the

> "Great chieftain o' the puddin' race,"

may he reign for ever! and when the tempting *plat* is before us, may we have strength of mind to stop before, a little before,

> "oor weel-swall'd kytes belyve
> Are bent like drums,
> . . . maist like to rive."

IX.

DRINK.

I CANNOT recall any allusion by Burns to water as a drink, nor any to whey or buttermilk, nor any to milk itself, except in connection with porridge:

> "Blest wi' content, and milk and meal;
> O leeze me on my spinning wheel."

Tea, besides being alluded to as a cause of war:

> "A'e nicht at tea began a plea
> Within America, man";

and as a source of taxation:

> "If he some scheme like tea and winnocks
> Wad kindly seek";

is alluded to as a beverage, but only for
"leddies":

> "Whiles o'er the wee bit cup an' platie,
> They sip the <u>scandal potion pretty</u>."

There is, of course, not a word of coffee, chocolate, etc.

<u>Of strong drink we have more than enough</u>. There are a few allusions to <u>wine</u>, of course not as a drink for common folk:

> "Poor plackless devils like mysel',
> It sets you ill
> Wi' bitter, dearthfu' wines to mell";

Captain Grose's drink is port:

> "Oh, port! oh, port! shine thou a wee,
> An' then ye'll see him";

and the Battle of the Whistle is fought in claret:

> "The dinner being over, the claret they ply."

Brandy has a hand in the disgraceful wind-up of the Holy Fair:

> "There's some are fou' o' brandy."

But Burns's patriotism and pocket both rise against the invader:

> "Wae worth that brandy, burning trash!
> Fell source o' mony a pain an' brash.
> 'T wins monie a poor, doylt, drucken hash,
> O' half his days,
> An' sends, besides, auld Scotland's cash
> To her warst faes."

The great drink was either whisky or beer in various forms, beer, the old national drink, being the commoner of the two. Whisky, which of late years has been displacing claret and champagne, had at one time nearly driven "the poor man's wine" from the field. Within my memory, a glass of draught beer could hardly be got in Scotland, and the only malt liquor in vogue was the pint bottle of sweet ale or hard porter, such as the pedestrian might find at a toll, or the mouthful of sma' yill with which the toper washed down his dram. It was whisky, whisky, everywhere. But whisky was not indigenous to the soil in which it took such firm root. The poisonous exotic came down on us from the Highlands—

the cruel avenger of the wrongs of the Celt. In Burns's day it was not fully naturalized: it is "a Highland gill," or "Usquebae," or "Ferintosh," or "that dear Kilbagie." And it has not yet got a firm footing in respectable society: it is the soldier's doxy that is "with usquebae an' blankets warm"; it is to cairds that we are to "gie yill and whisky . . . till they scunner." But it is in beer that the old comrades, over the memories of their boyhood, pledge each other:

> "An' surely ye'll be your pint stowp,
> An' surely I'll be mine."

Had the pint stowp (a Scotch pint) been filled with whisky, they would not have wanted a second. There are any number of varieties and of names of the old national drink. It is the "penny wheep," the "tippeny," the "nappy," the "yill," the "reaming swats." Porter also comes up once, at the Ordination, an orra drink on an orra occasion:

> "Come bouse about the porter."

Beer is drunk draught:

> "It's aye the cheapest lawyer's fee
> To taste the barrel."

As with whisky, which besides being drunk *au naturel* is made into toddy—

> "The four-gill chap we's gar him clatter,
> An' kirsen him wi' reekin' water"—

so with beer; besides being drunk fresh from the tap "in cheerful tankards foaming," it is drunk *hot-with*. Here is one of several instances:

> "That merry nicht we get the corn in,
> O sweetly then thou reams the horn in!
> Or reekin' on a New-Year's mornin'
>   In cog or bicker,
> An' just a wee drap sp'ritual burn in
>   An' gusty sucker!"

This is the hot-spiced ale of the English village pub. I think it is as extinct in Scotland as the use of beer to porridge. Home-brewing is also dead—Mr. Gladstone killed what survived of it—but when "Willie brew'd a peck o' maut," so common was the process that it had worked itself into the language in figure of speech:

> "Syne as ye brew, my maiden fair,
> Keep mind that ye maun drink the yill";

and

> "My barmie noddle's workin' prime,
> My fancy yerkit up sublime."

Willie would also find that merchants had imported hops for his use:

> ". . . prigging o'er hops and raisins."

Burns represents alcohol as the great resource in sorrow, and, indeed, at all times and on all occasions, sorrowful or joyous, at kirk or at market, among all sorts and conditions of men, rich or poor, lay or clerical, in moderation or not—mostly not. No Forbes Mackenzie then restrained excess, and we have a man, an old married farmer,

> ". . . at the Lord's house, e'en on Sunday,
> Drinkin' wi' Kirkton Jean till Monday."

Nay, the inability to drink is named among

the miseries of old age:

> "When ance life's day draws near the gloamin',
> Then farewell cheerful tankards foamin'
> An' social noise."

But one must not take for gospel all that poor Burns says. One would suppose that the general abuse of strong drink was worse then than now, that working folks, the mass of the people, drank more. I believe they drank much less, *teste* Burns himself: "the merry friendly country folks," who will "haud their Hallowe'en" to the end of time, have no strong drink but the one "social glass of strunt," with which they "part aff careerin', Fu' blithe that night"; and the cotter's "cheerfu' supper" is washed down by "the soupe, their only Hawkie does afford." But after making all allowances, it is clear that drunkenness was rife then where it would not now be tolerated. Burns could not have boasted that he had "been bitch fou' 'mang godly priests," or have written the "Holy Fair," if sobriety had been as much a matter of course as it is now among ministers of religion or those joining in its most sacred office; and he could not have written the "Whistle" if "wallowing in wine" had been looked on as disgraceful by the gentry.

Nothing in Burns is more instructive than this "Whistle," a truthful account, with names given, of a real incident. Three of the leading gentry of the country—two of them highly accomplished, and one of them a "high ruling elder"—deliberately set themselves to see which can drink most without falling off his chair; and Burns, if not actually present, is left to publish an account of the struggle.

The piece is not pleasant reading, but there is encouragement to be got out of it. The fight for the Whistle is as impossible now-a-days as bull-baiting or duelling. A man in the rank of Maxweltown, or Glenriddell, or Craigdarroch, or in a much lower rank, who should join such an orgie, or who should drink like Sir Walter's or Dean Ramsay's old lairds and lawyers, would be expelled from society. Even much milder excesses that were allowed within living memory are sternly forbidden, and the Classes, barring individuals here and there who are known and shunned, are sober.[1] This great improvement has been brought about not by Act of Parliament, but by a gradual improvement in principle and sentiment. Why should we despair of a like cause producing a like effect in those ranks of life where drunkenness is not yet under a severe social ban? Our lairds took to drinking last century—earlier vice ran in another channel—because the rise in rents found

---

[1] On the 13th January, 1837, the historical Peel Banquet was held here, the most notable political demonstration ever held in Scotland. Dr. Cleland has given us a full account of it (including the speech of one of the very few survivors—1897—young Mr. Gladstone, who responded to the toast of "The Conservative Constituencies of England"). The good doctor enumerates all the glories of the function, and among them this, that, "though port and sherry wines were served out without limit" from 1217 cut-glass decanters, yet not more than two or three out of the 3293 noblemen and gentlemen were tipsy, and these two or three were got quietly away. We have improved even upon the standard of 1837.—Cleland's *Peel Banquet*, p. 110.

them with no better way of spending their money than on the pleasures of the table. For a like reason our working people took to drinking when their wages rose on their hands. With the growth of higher tastes their drinking is on the wane, and it will die out in the one class as it has died out in the other.

But this is an impatient age, and the *mode du jour* is to fly at every turn to legislation, *i.e.* in plain English, to coercion. Coercion of the lawless to stop them from attacking the lives, the liberties, or the belongings of the citizens is the first function, the one absolutely essential function, of civil society; and the quantity and quality of it are fixed by *Messieurs les Assassins*, for the defence must always beat the attack. Coercion to save grown men from making fools of themselves, or from reaping the fruits of their folly, is another matter. It often fails of its immediate end, and it never fails to curtail harmless liberty, and to weaken the self-reliance which has been the making of us.

X.

CLASSES AND MASSES.

THE LANDED CLASS.

BURNS speaks with great contempt of these—
of their gluttony:

"... the gentry first are stechin";

"Gie dreepin' roasts to kintra lairds
Till icicles hing frae their beards";

of their dulness:

"There passes the squire and his brother the horse";

"Some gapin', glowrin' countra laird";

"Ye see yon birkie ca'd a lord,
He's but a cuif for a' that";

of their arrogance and their self-indulgence:

"They gang as saucy by puir folk,
As I wad by a stinkin' brock";

CLASSES AND MASSES 65

"I tent less, and want less
 Their roomy fireside,
But hanker and canker
 To see their cursed pride";

"Alas! how oft in haughty mood,
 God's creatures they oppress!
Or else, neglecting a' that's guid,
 They riot in excess."

And he describes the astonishing deference paid them:

"Or is't the paughty feudal Thane,
Wi' ruffled sark an' glancin' cane,
Wha thinks himsel' nae sheep-shank bane,
 But lordly stalks,
While caps and bannets aff are ta'en,
 As by he walks?"

even at "the sacrament" they are specially considered:

"There stands a shed to fend the showers,
 An' screen our country gentry":[1]

and Burns himself, though "not envying" the peer, "gives him his bow."

---

[1] Norman Macleod's father, "Old Norman" of St. Columba, in a graphic account of an open-air communion at Dūnvegan in 1824, tells us that "some of the better class had erected tents for their own use." *Memoir of Norman Macleod*, I. 338.

Those, we must remember, were the days of "slee Dundas," and for "saying aye or no's he bade them" in London, <u>the great Boss let our lords and lairds do as they liked in Scotland. Y<u>et</u></u> many of them, "in spite of all temptation," won Burns's own respect and affection. Here are some lairds:

Graham of Fintra:

> "The generous Graham";

Fergusson of Craigdarroch:

> "Craigdarroch, so famous for wit, worth, and law";

the Montgomeries of Coilsfield:

> ". . . a martial race portrayed
> In colours strong;
> Bold, soldier-featured, undismayed,
> They strode along";

William Wallace of Cairnhill:

> "And you farewell! whose merits claim
> Justly that highest badge to wear!
> Heaven bless your honour'd noble name,
> To masonry and Scotia dear!"

here is a baronet:

> "Thou who thy honour as thy God rever'st,
> Who, save thy mind's reproach, nought earthly fear'st";

here an earl :

> " Glencairn, the truly noble lies in dust,
> His country's pride, his country's stay " ;

here even a duke :

> " My Lord, I know your noble ear
> Woe ne'er assails in vain."

And when, not ill-pleased at the invitation and not quite at ease as to his comportment, he " dinner'd " with " the noble youthful Daer," Burns found he had to correct views taken at a distance :

> " The fient a pride, nae pride had he,
> Nor sauce nor state that I could see,
> Mair than an honest ploughman."

There are philosophers, a whole school of them, wall-eyed, narrow-nebbit, preposterous,

> " A set o' dull, conceited hashes,
> Plain truth to speak,"

who solemnly pile all the virtues on one class, and all the vices on another. Burns, when it comes to the bit, pushes this stuff aside, and tells us that God hath made of one blood all classes as well as all nations of men.

THE MIDDLE CLASS.

If Burns has a good word for the Gentry, he has never a one for the Merchandry. They are sordid purse-proud rogues; they are

> "The warldly race that drudge and drive";

> "The warldly race that riches chase";

> "The selfish warldly race
> Wha think that havins sense and grace,
> E'en love an' friendship should gie place
> To catch the plack";

> "The sly men of business contriving a snare";

> "There centum per centum, the cit with his purse."

(Ah, me! the profits of those days!)

> "Poor centum per centum may fast,
> And grumble his hurdies their claithing;
> He'll find, when the balance is cast,
> He's gane to the devil for—naething."

> "Do ye envy the city gent
> Behind a kist to lie an' sklent,
> Or purse-proud, big wi' cent per cent,
> An' muckle wame,
> In some bit brugh to represent
> A Bailie's name?"

> "The cit and polecat stink and are secure."

CLASSES AND MASSES

There's a banning for you ! "'This is a sad curse,' said my father. ' I am sorry for it,' quoth my Uncle Toby." But Burns knew little of the class he denounced. Had he known them better, had he "dinner'd" more with them, he would have found that there were as good men ahint a kist, *i.e.* counter, as ahint a plough. On his own showing, his own class, men and women, old and young could be as sordid as any of them.

"Master Tootie" of Mauchline is an adept in tricks,

> "Like scrapin' out auld Crummie's nicks,
> An' tellin' lies about them";

Lowrie, the Laird o' Drumeller,

> "He brags and he blaws o' his siller"

as loud as could your city gent ; Corydon looks as sharp to the *dot* as any French bourgeois :

> " O gie me the lass that has acres o' charms,
> O gie me the lass wi' the weel stockit farms";

Jenny's mother compels her daughter to marry money as calmly as if she lived in Mayfair:

> " Bad luck to the penny that tempted my minnie,
> To sell her poor Jenny for siller and lan' ! "

Meg o' the Mill needs no compelling:

> " She has gotten a cuif wi' a claute o' siller,
> And broken the heart o' the barley miller " ;

and blythe Bessie at the milking shiel is cautioned to

> "cannie wale
> A routhie but, a routhie ben.
> . . . . .
> Tak' this frae me, my bonnie hen,
> Its plenty beets the luver's fire."

I am no judge of Arcadies, but, as far as I can make out, as fine specimens of the *Genus Sordidum* are to be found in the lower strata as in the upper.

It is some comfort to traders to note that Burns thinks quite as meanly of lawyers. " Godly writers," indeed, are named, but as

> " Dear remembered ancient yealings,
> And what would now be strange."

Their present representatives are "druken writers"; they

> ". . . ply every art of legal thieving,"

and the diabolical reliquary of Kirk Alloway includes

> "Three lawyers' tongues, turned inside out,
> Wi' lies seam'd like a beggar's clout."

Happily, the blackness even here is relieved by Gaun Hamilton:

> "What's no his ain he winna tak' it;
> What aince he says he winna break it;
> As master, landlord, husband, father,
> He doesna fail his part in either!"

The factor comes off very badly. "Puir tenant bodies, scant o' cash," have to "thole his snash," his oaths, and his threats. Nay, worse:

> "There's mony a creditable stock
> O' decent, honest, fawsont fo'k
> Are riven out baith root an' branch,
> Some rascal's pridefu' greed to quench,
> Wha thinks to knit himsel' the faster
> In favour wi' some gentle Master."

The doctor is surgeon and apothecary as well.

> "And then o' doctor's saws and whittles,
> O' a' dimensions, shapes, an' mettles,
> A' kinds o' boxes, mugs, and bottles,
> He's sure to hae."

There is a surveyor of taxes, fortunately for us, for to his Schedule we owe "The Inventory," with all it tells of old farm life.

The illicit distiller follows his calling under sore disabilities from "those d—mn'd excisemen." Burns sympathizes with the patriotic industrial, fighting against the Lon'on parliament's

> ". . . curst restrictions
> On Aqua Vitae."

On the other hand, he denounces the oversea contrabandist, the "blackguard smuggler," for tempting

> "Poor plackless bodies like himsel',
> Wi' bitter dearthfu' wines to mell,
> Or foreign gill."[1]

---

[1] Well might Burns denounce the "blackguard smuggler." It was he who initiated him, a lad of sixteen, in "scenes of swaggering riot and roaring dissipation."—See *Autobiography*. Paterson's *Burns*, IV. 12.

Now-a-days the illicit distiller has retired to the corries of Ross and Sutherland, and the "chuffie vintner" no longer "colleagues" with the illicit importer. But I suppose the vintner's laugh is "ready chorus" still to a good customer's "queerest stories." I hope his wife no longer pushes her wares by the arts of Tam o' Shanter's landlady.

The pawnbroker hangs up the three balls, as he does to-day, alongside the vintner:

> "Gude ale gars me sell my hose,
> Sell my hose, an' pawn my shoon."

The miller is often named: every barony had its mill. The mill is a sort of club:

> "At kirk or market, mill or smiddie,"

Caesar, though he is "o' high degree," forgathers with the "tawted tyke"; and

> "Ilka melder wi' the miller,"

Tam o' Shanter

> "Sits as lang as he has siller."

"Brewer Gabriel's fire" has once blazed,

and the browster wife "brew'd gude ale for gentlemen."

The maltster is implied by "John Barleycorn," and the distiller by "thae cursed horse-leeches o' the Excise."

There is no baker; why should there be in the "Land o' cakes" and "souple scones, the wale o' food"? But the butcher is known:

"... as butchers like a knife";

and the barber—he dresses the gentles' heads:

"Men three parts made by Taylors and by Barbers."

There is no watch or clock maker; the pocket watch and the house clock, even the cheery little wag-at-the-wa', are modern luxuries. The only clocks named are the two clocks of Ayr, "the drowsy Dungeon Clock" and "Wallace Tower's."

The middleman scarce existed: there was no demand for him. People's wants were few, and were mostly supplied from their own labours,

"Wi' sma' to sell an' less to buy."

The traveller, bagman, or rider is not named. The "hops and raisins," the "gusty succar," the "succar candie," and the "wee bit cup and platie" do imply the grocer, but he is not named, nor the draper, nor the retailer of any sort.

The travelling "merchant" does most of the work of our shopkeeper. He is of two sorts: the chapman (*i.e. Kaufmann*), the aristocrat of the road, who deals in cambrics, ribbons, needles, knives, and garters; and the cadger, who deals in coarser goods, as crockery. The chapman carries his pack on his back; the cadger has perforce a beast of some sort. These men have a hard and rough life. "Market days are wearing late" and the chance of sales over, before the "Chapman billie leaves the street," and as he "trudges wi' his pack" across country, he may, even in sight of the market town, be "smoor'd" in the snaw; and it may be the cadger's fate as well as his pownie's to die "at some dyke back."

The schoolmaster is abroad:

"Gie him the schulin' o' your weans";

but Burns does not think much of him:

"What's a' your jargon o' your schools?
Leeze me on drink! it gies us mair
Than either school or college."

Burns speaks with a shudder of "vampire booksellers" and "scorpion critics," but it was not in the land of Burns that these creatures bled or bit.

THE WORKING CLASS.

In old days operations were simple, and labour little subdivided, and several sorts of workers now everywhere to be found, do not appear in Burns's poems. There are no masons (except Freemasons), and no slaters: biggish farmers are content to live in "auld clay biggans," roofed with "thack and rape." There are of course no plumbers or glaziers, painters or paperhangers. It is more curious to find no wright, joiner, or carpenter; but the tools and training needed for rough woodwork are within a layman's reach.

On the other hand, ironworking, from the tools and training it needs, is always a separate trade.

> "An' Burnewin comes on like death
> At every chap!"

Burnewin is also farrier:

> "An' every naig was ca'd a shoe on,
> The smith and Tam got roarin' fou on."

With her "spinning wheel," or her simpler "rock and reel," any lass can make lint or "oo" into yarn, but the weaver or wabster is an artist. He often appears, and is of two sorts. There is the customer weaver like Willie Wastle, who wove you a web from your own yarn (or part of it):

> "Willie was a wabster gude,
> Cou'd stown a clue wi' ony bodie";

and the trade weaver, like

> "... the batch o' wabster lads
> Blackguardin' frae Kilmarnock,"

where the carpet trade has already taken root.

The weaver begets the heckler:[1]

"O merry ha'e I been teething a heckle."

We have the shoemaker in the immortal Soutar Johnny.

And the customer taylor makes up your own cloth for you on the ethical lines of Willie Wastle:

"The Taylor staw the linin' o't."

There are no dyers or bleachers, but my "waukit loof" finely indicates the fuller's art.

The "collier laddie" is already scratching at the rich Ayrshire coal field.

---

[1] It would have been well for Burns had he never heard of the heckler's trade. It was when learning it at Irvine that he met Richard Brown, and it was Richard Brown who taught him to "look with levity on a certain fashionable failing which hitherto I had regarded with horror." His new friend's teaching soon bore fruit, as Burns himself tells, in the seduction of Elizabeth Paton.—*Autobiography*, Paterson, IV. 15.

The "land labourer" naturally appears in many lights. He ploughs,

> "The brawny, bany, ploughman chiel";

he sows,

> "With joy the tentie seedsman stalks";

he reaps,

> "Our stibble rig was Rab M'Graen";

he threshes with

> ". . . the weary flingin' tree":

he has to turn his hand to rough work,

> "An' sometimes a-hedgin' an' ditchin' I go";

or we find him

> "Wi' dirty stanes biggin' a dyke,
> Barin' a quarry an' sic like";

or, at odd hours, he

> ". . . sneds besoms, thraws saugh woodies";

or, *fortunatum nimium!* he may be sent to the hill, where he has his chance of "guid fat braxies," and,

> "Where nature smiles as sweet, I ween,
> To shepherds as to kings."

There is lighter work for boys. Burns has three of them at Mossgiel,

"Run deils for rantin' and for noise!"

One is "a gaudsman," one "a thresher," and wee Davock has only to "haud the nowt in fother." Sawney, poor Meg's Hallowe'en escort, has even lighter work than Davock: he has but to "herd the kye" on the Out-field.

Several maidens grieve over the absence, not unnatural, of their "sailor lads," of whom one runs a double risk,

"He's on the seas to meet the foe";

and there is one allusion, only one, to sea-fishers. Caesar the Great has been

"... whalpit somewhere far abroad,
Where sailors gang to fish for cod."

Of the gentry's personal servants we have three:

"His flunkies answer at the bell";

"His whipper-in, wee blastit wonner";

and (like master like man),

"The groom gat sae fu' he fell awalt beside it."

The "Minister's man" appears in his alternative quality as "Auld Clinkumbell."

Strolling performers, Burns names as a discredited class. But the hard life of the "mountebank squad" has his sympathy:

> "Poor Andrew that tumbles for sport,
>   Let naebody name wi' a jeer;
> There's even, I'm tauld, i' the Court,
>   A tumbler ca'd the Premier."

The immigration from the Highlands had scarce begun: Highland Mary is its only representative. "My gallant braw John Hielandman" has been rather in us than of us:

> "He ranged a' from Tweed to Spey";
> "An' lalland laws he held in scorn";

and when the "raucle carlin" sings his praise, he has left us for good:

> "They've hanged my braw John Hielandman."

The immigration from Ireland had not begun, and there was probably not an Irishman in Ayrshire; none at least are named.

Girls we find employed much like country girls now. They do the work of the house at home:

"An' aye she wrought her mammy's wark";

they "bleach their claes" or "wash the ploughman's hose"; or they are

"At service out amang the neighbours roun'";

perhaps they are, like Blythe Bessie, "at the milking shiel," and "plunge and plunge the kirn" for the "yellow treasure"; or they work in the fields:

"Still shearin' and clearin'
The tither stookit raw."

But besides all this, we find them at work at which we should not find their successors,

"At rock an' reel an' spinnin' wheel";

"O leeze me on my spinning wheel!
O leeze me on my rock an' reel!
Frae tap to tae that cleeds me bien,
An' haps me biel an' warm at e'en."

The rock—one can still see the nimble-fingered Italian women sitting at it on the doorstep in the sun—is a picturesque implement; but spinning with the rock, or even with the wheel, is a slow process, and many a girl, before she had done " her dizzens," before

> " The cardin' o't, the spinnin' o't,
> The warpin' o't, the winnin' o't,"

were all got through, might groan out

> " The weary pund, the weary pund,
> The weary pund o' tow."

Knitting is in full force:

> " On fasten e'en we had a rockin',
> To ca' the crack, and weave our stockin'."

There is no notice of milliner or mantua-maker, tho' " twa manteeles o' dolefu' black " and Jenny's " braw new gown " appear.

The list of workers ends with the keeper of

> " Death's unlovely, dreary, dark abode ! "

" Johnny Ged's Hole," utilized above ground as well as under,

> " The braw calf-ward where gowans grew
> Sae white an' bonnie."

THE NON-WORKING CLASS.

The non-workers, tramps and others with minds made up never with their goodwill to do one honest day's work, these, like the honest poor, we have always with us, but the volume of dregs is much reduced: we have clarified the residuum. Burns's marvellous picture of Poosie Nansie's would scarce be true of our lowest doss-house.

Tinkers and gypsies, an ugly breed now almost extinct, constantly appear. We have

"The gypsy gang that deal in glamour!"

Willie Wastle's handsome wife,

"Oh, Tinkler Madgie was her mither!"

Caesar makes love to

". . . a tinkler-gipsey's messin";

and Poosie Nansie's guests include a "tinker hizzie" and a "sturdy caird," "a tinker to his station."

Begging is now a decaying and discredited

industry. Burns shows it as so common that, as we have seen, beggar's or "poke-meal" is a regular article of commerce. And begging is nothing to be ashamed of. It may be a mere way of speaking when Burns tells a brother poet

> ". . . the Muse, she'll never leave ye
>   Tho' e'er sae puir,
> Na e'en tho' limpin' wi' the spavie
>   Frae door to door";

or says of himself,

> ". . . tho' I should beg
>   Wi' lyart pow,
> I'll laugh an' sing an' shake my leg
>   As lang's I dow";

but he does seemingly contemplate without dismay the actual possibility of having to live by begging:

> "For, Lord be thankit, I can plough,
> And when I downa yoke a naig,
> Then, Lord be thankit, I can beg";

and again,

> "Mair spier na, nor fear na,
>   Auld age ne'er mind a feg,
> The last o't, the warst o't,
>   Is only but to beg."

The respectability of begging, to this day hard to kill, was kept in life by the survival of the official beggar, like Edie Ochiltree. Burns speaks of himself as

> "about to beg a pass for leave to beg,"

and describes hypocrisy as

> ". . . the blue-gown badge an' claithing
> O' saunts."

XI.

THE CHURCH.

I DO not ask what might be gathered or inferred from Burns as to the spiritual forces then at work in Scotland, but only what he tells us as to ecclesiastical conditions and arrangements.

And here the first thing that strikes one is the keen interest shown in such matters. Now-a-days a man of Burns's cast of mind would pass by in contemptuous silence the Church, its creeds, its customs, its quarrels, and would waste no time over your " Kirk's Alarms," or " Holy Fairs," or " Twa Herds." But in Burns's Scotland no matters commanded such keen general interest as Church matters.

It had long been so. ⌈It was the Church, not the State, that had made the Scotch Reformation. It was the Church that had led the long struggle, partly religious, partly political, against tyranny. It was through the Church Courts that religious, national, and popular sentiment found vent: Scotland had never had a Parliament such as England's, and long after the Union, Scotland, poor and isolated, took little interest in the doings of "the folk in Lon'on":⌋ it was over the doings of her Church Courts, their Governments and their Oppositions, their overtures and their debates, that the eager race were eager. Burns himself could never resist a theological discussion:

> "Your pardon, sir, for this digression,
> But when divinity comes 'cross me
> My readers still are sure to lose me."

Of the Church Courts he names only two—the Kirk Session:

> "Wi' pinch, I put a Sunday's face on,
> An' snoov'd awa' before the Session";

and the Presbytery:

> " Lord, hear my earnest cry and prayer
> Against the Presbyt'ry of Ayr."

There was work going on all the while in the Synod at Glasgow, and in the General Assembly at Edinburgh; but it was a long day's journey to Glasgow, a long two days' journey to Edinburgh, and newspapers were an unknown luxury. In the very heat of the French Revolution, Burns, a farmer and an exciseman, gets a reading of a newspaper. Here is what the favour means to him:

> " Kind Sir, I've read your paper through,
> And, faith, to me 'twas really new!
> How guessed ye, Sir, what maist I wanted?
> This mony a day I've grain'd and gaunted
> To ken what French mischief was brewin',
> Or what the drumlie Dutch were doin'.
> . . . . . .
> A' this and mair I never heard of;
> And, but for you, I might despair'd of.
> So gratefu', back your news I send you,
> And pray a' gude things may attend you."

There is a significant disproportion in Burns's frequent Biblical allusions. These, with scarce an exception, take us to the Old Testament. It was on this part of the Bible that old Scotch preachers mainly dwelt, and Burns reflects their teaching. He occasionally uses the word "Christian," but only twice does he make it appear that he has ever seen inside the New Testament—once in his ill-natured "Epigram on a Country Laird":

> "Bless Jesus Christ, O Cardoness,
>   With grateful lifted eyes,
> Who taught that not the soul alone,
>   But *body* too, shall rise!"

once in "The Cotter's Saturday Night":

> "Perhaps the Christian volume is the theme,
> How guiltless blood for guilty man was shed."

There are, to be sure, one or two allusions to Baptism. In the "horrible and awfu'" collection that

> "heroic Tam was able,
> To note upon the Haly Table,"

were

> "Twa span-lang, wee, unchristen'd bairns";

and when "at Mauchline Race or Mauchline Fair," Burns shall meet Lapraik,

> "The four-gill chap, we'se gar him clatter,
> And kirs'n him wi' reekin' water!"

There is no allusion whatever to "the Sacrament," *i.e.* the Communion—not even in the "Holy Fair."

The great Church function, the special work of the minister, is preaching:

> "Ye ministers, come mount the pupit,
> An' cry, till ye be haerse an' rupit,
> For eighty-eight he wish'd ye weel,
> An' gied ye a' baith gear an' meal."

But preaching is not what it has been.

> "Nae langer Rev'rend Men, their country's glory,
> In plain braid Scots hold forth a plain braid story";

> "What signifies his barren shine
> Of moral pow'rs and reason?
> His English style, and gesture fine,
> Are a' clean oot o' season."

Even Ritualism is creeping in:

> "Some quarrel the Presbyter gown." [1]

---

[1] Ministers also practise hair powder:
> "Some mim-mou'd, pouther'd priestie,
> Wi' band upon his breastie."

Well into this century the 'rags of Poperie' were a stone of stumbling and rock of offence to the stricter

Alas, was there no Jacob Primmer to "nip the poison in the bud"?

Presbyterians. Hear an Auld Licht Anti-Burgher Seceder on the ritualism of the New Lichts:

> "Ha, ha! Seceders, brag nae mair
> O' your pretended zeal and care:
> Ye hae o' pride as large a share
>   As ither folk:
> Your priests wear bands, an' pouther'd hair,
>   An' sic vain troke.
>
> "Wow! what would Ralph and Eben say,
> Had they been livin' at this day?
> To see them clad in sic array,
>   Wi' gown and bands;
> They would exclaim (as weel they may),
>   Ah! sinfu' lands!
>
> . . . . .
>
> "For now they are conformin' fast.
> They first wore bands, and, now that's past,
>   Each wears a gown;
> Reading comes next, an' then at last
>   Their zeal fa's down."

"Reading" means use of MS. in preaching. "Ralph and Eben" are the Secession Fathers, Ralph and Ebenezer Erskine. As late as 1821, a member of Kirk Session of the Old Light Burgher Seceders of Glasgow seceded with his family, because his new minister, the Rev. Michael Willis, wore gown and bands which had been presented to him on his settlement.—*Annals of the Original Seceders*, by the Rev. David Scott, D.D., p. 593.

THE CHURCH

Public prayer is in use to be asked for the sick:

"Auld Orthodoxy . . .
. . . fetches at the thrapple,
An' fechts for breath;
Haste, gie her name up in the chappel,
Nigh unto death."

In Burns's Scotland, Nonconformity was of small account. In all his Church allusions there is scarce one but to the Established Church.

Episcopacy appears once:

"Some quarrel Episcopal graithing";

"The Paip's Church" once:

"yon paughty dog
That bears the keys of Peter";

and once

"Black gowns of each denomination."

Seceders and Relievers, Burghers and Anti-Burghers, had long been at work—good, quiet work—in Ayr, Kilmarnock, and Dumfries, but they are contemptuously ignored.[1]

---

[1] I need scarce say that the Auld Kirk "New Lichts" of the Ordination, etc., are not the correlates of the

Not clerics only lead the offices of religion. Heads of families were held bound, under pain of Church discipline, to keep up the "Familie Exercise" morning and evening. We have the full order of this Exercise, as we should have had it round the ingle of William Burness:

1. From the Psalms of David in metre (Rous's version) they sing, to some old Scotch tune that ". . . beets the heav'nward flame,"

"Those strains that once did sweet in Zion glide";

2. "The priest-like father reads the sacred page";

Ultra-Seceder "Auld Lichts" that brighten Barrie's pages. Burns's "New Lichts" were the broad, very broad, party in the Established Church. They were brand new in his day. Replying in 1785 to "Winsome Willie," he says:

"Ye bade me write you what they mean
By this *New-Light*,"

and he adds this foot-note: "*New Light* is a cant phrase in the West of Scotland for those religious opinions which Dr. Taylor of Norwich has defended strenuously."

3. "Then kneeling down to Heaven's Eternal King,
   The saint, the husband, and the father prays."[1]

But not all heads of families take as kindly to their duty as William Burness—not, for one, his son Robert:

"For prayin', I ha'e little skill o't;
I'm baith dead sweer, an' wretched ill o't."

This implies, I take it, that Burns did in some sort submit to conduct the "Familie Exercise" at Mossgiel. He certainly did give in to teach

---

[1] See Edgar's *Old Church Life in Scotland*, 1st series, page 203. "Habitual," if not total, neglect "of family worship" was one of the charges laid against Gavin Hamilton by the Kirk Session of Mauchline in January, 1785. It is to be noted that at the previous autumn Sacrament, Hamilton, along with several other Mauchline members, had been delated to the Kirk Session for neglect of ordinances, and had submitted to a private admonition by the Kirk Session before he could get his Communion token. See a full report of the proceedings in *Robert Burns and the Ayrshire Moderates* (privately printed, 1883). Edgar, one of our best authorities on our old Church life, is an exceptional authority on Burns in that he was minister of Mauchline.

the Shorter Catechism to his three "run deils":

> "An' aye on Sundays, duly, nightly,
> I on the questions tairge them tightly;
> Till, faith, wee Davock's turn'd sae gleg,
> Tho' scarcely langer than your leg,
> He'll screed you aff Effectual Calling
> As fast as ony in the dwalling."

Private prayer is well established. The cotter enjoins it on his children:

> "An' O! be sure to fear the Lord alway,
> An' mind your *duty* duly morn an' night";

and he practises what he preaches:

> "The parent-pair their secret homage pay,
> And proffer up to heaven the warm request.'

Sometimes the oratory is the open air. Burns represents his granny as retiring from the noise of the house

> "To say her prayers, douce, honest woman!
> Ayont the dyke."

Grace is said, both before meat:

> "I'll sit down o'er my scanty meal,
> Be't water brose or muslin kail,
>   Wi' cheerfu' face—
> As lang's the Muses dinna fail—
>   To say the grace";

and after meat:

> "Then auld guidman, maist like to rive,
> *Be thankit* hums."

The grace is sometimes "fu' lang." Burns speaks of

> "Three-mile prayers and half-mile graces."

He has left us several terse both before-meat and after-meat graces, notably the admirable "Selkirk grace":

> "Some ha'e meat, and canna eat,
>   And some wad eat that want it;
> But we ha'e meat, and we can eat,
>   And sae the Lord be thankit."

XII.

CHURCH PATRONAGE.

CHURCH Patronage deserves a paragraph to itself. Church patronage must be a puzzler to those simple souls who think by the book, and take for granted that an institution will everywhere work in the same way. In England, where advowsons have been as freely bought and sold as consols, patronage has brought little trouble on the Church. In Scotland, where there has at least been no simony, it has vexed the Church from Queen Anne to Queen Victoria. It stirs the wrath of Burns's cotters:

"They'll talk o' patronage an' priests
Wi' kindling fury in their breasts";

and it makes godly ministers groan:

CHURCH PATRONAGE

> "Lang patronage, wi' rod o' airn,
> Has shor'd the Kirk's undoing."

It is dead and buried now, but from its grave it shores it still. The Church was taunted with patronage: it was a disability to her, a clog on her work, a yoke that neither our fathers nor we were able to bear. She threw off the yoke, and her very freedom, the new life it might breathe into her, has been the signal for a disestablishment campaign by a sister Church, the Church of Chalmers!

One might have expected Burns on general principles to take the popular side as against patronage. But Burns was one of those commonplace characters who repudiate General Principles, however Grand, as guides in affairs. He judged an institution by the way it worked, and to his thinking patronage worked excellently well. The "orthodox, orthodox" school of ministers had no love of patronage: nay, they threatened its supporters,

> "If mair they deave us wi' their din
> O' patronage intrusion";

and they looked for preferment to popular support :

> "Ye wha were ne'er by lairds respeckit
> To wear the plaid,
> But by the brutes themselves eleckit
> To be their guide."

It was Burns's friends, the New Lichts, who leant on patrons, and Burns would never with his good-will see

> "The brutes have power themselves
> To chose their herds."

XIII.

CHURCH DISCIPLINE.

ALONGSIDE of the civil courts, ecclesiastical courts, especially Kirk Sessions, exercised a co-ordinate jurisdiction, not merely over church offences, as swearing, sabbath-breaking, neglect of ordinances, drunkenness, impurity, but over petty civil offences, as brawls, slanders, thefts, assaults.[1] The system, like other systems,

---

[1] Even murder was dealt with by the Church Courts. By an act of the General Assembly of 1648, a murderer, "in case the magistrate do not do his duty in punishing the crime capitally," was first to confess his sin before both the Session and the Presbyterie, and there to show some signs of repentance, and was thereafter to "make public profession of repentance" before the congregation, clothed in sackcloth for fifty-two Sabbaths. It was only by Act of Parliament passed after the Revolution that

had its goods and its ills in it. Nothing could be worse than the Kirk Session's *police des mœurs* in cases of impurity: the cruel exposure hardened the hardened offender, and drove the blush from the face of the girl still blushing for her fall.[1] But in the absence of the machinery that now-a-days controls crime great or small, it was well that there was some court always at hand to take up petty offenders. Kirk Sessions did not hesitate to issue sentences—the jougs, fines, imprisonment, banishment from the parish—that they had no power to enforce; but to meet the case of contumacious panels they were in use to have in their number a 'Session Bailie' (specially named by the sheriff), or an ordinary bailie

---

excommunication absolutely ceased to carry with it any liability to civil penalties, escheat or caption. Edgar, 1st series, pp. 198 n., 245 *et seq.*; *Acts of the General Assembly*, Edinburgh, 1843, p. 193.

[1] There is reason to think that the dread by poor girls of the shameful exposure on the stool of repentance led to a good deal of child murder. Aiton's *Survey of Ayrshire*, quoted by Edgar, 1st series, p. 323 n.

CHURCH DISCIPLINE

or justice of the peace, who, as a magistrate, enforced the sentence he had just issued as an elder. In one case that we know, the Kirk Session sentenced a strolling clown to the jougs and to the cutty stool. Besides being an outsider, the man could not for the life of him see where the harm was:

> "I ance was tied up like a stirk
> For civilly swearing and quaffing;
> I ance was abused in the kirk
> For towzling a lass i' my daffing."

In such a case a little civil pressure may have been wanted. But generally the Kirk Session was herself sufficient for these things. She could cast out of the synagogue, and few dared to face this tremendous weapon.[1] It brought Burns himself to his knees. We know the fact otherwise, but we can gather

---

[1] The old phrase was that the offender, after penance and absolution, was again "received in the societie of the kirk as ane lyvely member thereof."—*Booke of the Universall Kirk of Scotland.*

as much from his poems. Alluding to his seduction of Elizabeth Paton, he says:

> "An' then, if kirk folks dinna clutch me,
> I ken the devils dare nae touch me";

The kirk folks do clutch him, and he submits at once, "pays the fee," "a gowd guinea," and, worse than that,

> "Tholes their blethers";

he makes Elizabeth Paton, or some other victim of his lust, say:

> "When I mount the creepie chair,
> Wha will sit beside me there?
> Gie me Rob, I seek nae mair,
> The rantin' dog, the daddie o't";

among his familiar troubles he gives:

> "O' a' the numerous human dools,
> Ill hairsts, daft bargains, cutty stools";

and as the natural sequel, whether to himself or to some one else, of "mooping wi' the servant hizzie," he names,

> "Stand i' the stool when I hae dune."

In that vile piece, "What ails ye now, ye lousie bitch?" he professes to

"   .   .   .   tell for sport,
How he did wi' the Session sort."

His conduct, as he paints the scene, is beyond measure shocking, but the thing never happened. The "blasphemy and bawdry," Scott Douglas's own words, are Burns's poor revenge for the humiliations he dared not refuse.[1]

---

[1] In the "Extempore to Mr. Gavin Hamilton" (first published by Alexander Smith) Burns writes thus:

"The priest anathémas may threat—
Predicament, Sir, that we're baith in;
But when honour's reveillé is beat,
The holy artillery's naething."

These brave lines Scott Douglas (Paterson's *Burns*, I. 336) assigns to "about August, 1786." But on 6th August, 1786, Burns "stood" for the third time in Mauchline Church, and, "making profession for repentance for ye sin of fornication," was publicly rebuked and thereon absolved. Edgar (2nd Series, p. 401 n.) gives the Minute from the Kirk Session Records and a copy of the Rebuke.

XIV.

CRIMINAL JURISPRUDENCE.

For an Arcadian district, the Land of Burns has a respectable record of crime, even allowing for the special contributions of "randie gangrel bodies."

We have offences against the person—murder simple:

"A murderer's banes in gibbet airns";

parricide:

"A knife a father's throat had mangled,
Whom his ain son o' life bereft";

infanticide, twice:

"A garter which a babe had strangled";

and,

"the cairn
Whare hunters fand the murderer'd bairn."

If we take as correct Burns's account of the morality of his district, we may expect a good deal of infanticide.

We have offences against property—thieving:

> "As eager runs the market crowd
> When 'Catch the thief' resounds aloud";

pocket picking:

> "a raucle carlin
> Wha kent fu' weel to cleek the sterling."

We have smaller offenders—
the law-breaker on principle:

> "The lalland laws he held in scorn";

and the chronic deserter:

> "I've ta'en the gold, I've been enroll'd
> In mony a noble squadron,
> But vain they search'd, when off I march'd
> To go an' clout the caudron."

If crime thrives, it is not that justice is mealy-mouthed—
they hang for stealing:

> "A thief new cuttit frae a rape";

they hang a murderer in chains:

"A murderer's banes in gibbet airns";

they hang for pure cussedness:

"They've hanged my braw John Highlandman";

they hang till hanging is always cropping up in their talk:

"Then orthodoxy yet may prance,
An' learning in a woody dance";

"Wae worth the man that first did shape
That vile, wanchancie thing—a rape!"

"But gude preserve us frae the gallows,
That shamefu' death";

"The timmer is scant, when ye're ta'en for a saunt,
Wha should hang in a rape for an hour."

and it is taken for granted that the arch-executioner hangs like Braxfield:

"Hear me, auld *Hangie*, for a wee,
And let poor damn'd bodies be."

They do sometimes condescend on lighter punishments. We have the frowsy cells

"Where tiny thieves, not destin'd yet to swing,
Beat hemp for others, riper for the string";

before they came to the hanging of my braw John Highlandman they had

"... banished him beyond the sea";

his friend, the raucle carlin, had

"... in mony a well been dookit";

and other offenders had had to

"... herd the buckskin kye
    For 't in Virginia."

The hangman flogs as well as hangs:

"The fear of hell's a hangman's whup,"

which whup he flourished here in Glasgow as late as 1822.[1]

In Burns's day they imprisoned for debt:

"But smash them, crash them, a' to spails,
An' rot the dyvors in the jails."

---

[1] On 8th May, 1822, Richard Campbell was whipped by the hangman through the town of Glasgow, twenty lashes each at the Jail, the Stockwell-foot, the Stockwell-head, and the Cross. Campbell's whole offence (for which he had also fourteen years' transportation) was taking part in a riot at the Dreghorn Mansion, where the mob believed a boy had been foully murdered. On 25th September, 1793, Mary Douglas was whipped through the town for housebreaking.—*Regality Club*, 1st Series, p. 65. *Glasgow Past and Present* (1884), I. 339.

In those last sad days at Brow, Burns, in terror of imprisonment by a "cruel scoundrel of a haberdasher," wrote to George Thomson and James Burness those piteous appeals for a small loan. To understand his terror, one must remember that the *squalor carceris* was in Scotch law a recognized means of torturing the debtor into payment, and that our old Tolbooths were thoroughly in keeping with our old law.[1]

---

[1] See "Auld Ayr" for a description of the Tolbooth of Ayr. See also Hugo Arnot's appalling picture of the Heart of Midlothian. Effie Deans is the only prisoner, as far as known, who ever refused to escape from its foul *oubliettes*. How the refusal brings home to us the girl's hopeless misery!

XV.

SUPERSTITIONS.

BURNS'S poems, especially "Tam o' Shanter," the "Address to the Deil," and "Hallowe'en," are full of notices of superstitious beliefs. We have the foul Thief himself, and his acolytes, witches and warlocks, ghaists and goblins, fays and bogles;

" . . . water kelpies haunt the foord,"

and

"moss-traversing spunkies
Decoy the wight that late and drunk is."

It is not easy to say how much all these were really believed in, but some belief in them there certainly was. Not Merran only "swat" and poor Meg "ran through midden hole and a'" in their terror at the Hallowe'en portents, but the sturdy Rab M'Graen

> "For mony a day was by himsel',
> He was sae sairly frighted
> That vera nicht";

and "fechtin' Jamie Fleck"

> "Roared a horrid murder shout,
> An' tumbled wi' a wintle,
> Out-owre that night."

It is to be noted that the scene of "Hallowe'en" is laid, not near the town of Ayr, but in the wilder uplands,

> "Amang the bonnie winding banks
> Where Doon rins, wimplin', clear."

The old beliefs were falling back into the Hinterland, as weaker races fall back before the invader.

XVI.

POLITICS.

BURNS wrote during the meanest epoch of our history, when the government of Scotland was cruel, corrupt, wasteful, and "her chosen Five and Forty,"

> "Ye Irish Lords, ye Knights an' Squires,
> Wha represent our brughs an' shires,"

were chosen without a pretence of popular election, and were mostly in the pay, by "pension, post, or place," of

> "... a chap that's d–mn'd auld farran,
> Dundas his name."

The vile state of things comes plainly out in Burns. When the simple Luath excuses the absentee laird,

> "aiblins thrang a-parliamentin',
> For Britain's guid his saul indentin',"

Caesar breaks in:

> "Haith, lad, ye little ken about it:
> For Britain's guid! guid faith! I doubt it.
> Say rather, gaun as Premiers lead him,
> An' saying aye or no's they bid him.
>
> . . . . . .
>
> For Britain's guid! for her destruction!
> Wi' dissipation, feud, an' faction!"

Among "Scotia's race" as Burns sees them in the "Vision,"

> "Some fire the Soldier on to dare;
> Some rouse the Patriot up to bare
>   Corruption's heart.
>
> . . . . . .
>
> "Or 'mid the venal Senate's roar
>   They, sightless, stand,
> To mend the honest Patriot lore,
>   An' grace the land."

He exhorts "the chosen Five and Forty":

> "Let posts or pensions sink or soom
>   Wi' them wha grant them:
> If honestly they canna come,
>   Far better want them";

and appeals to King George himself to

> "rax Corruption's neck
> An' gi'e her for dissection."

XVII.

TAXATION.

TAXATION is whipped up to keep pace with the unresting advance of expenditure. All Britain groans:

> "Your sair taxation does her fleece
> Till she has scarce a tester";

Scotland is even harder pressed,

> "An' plundered o' her hindmost groat
> By gallows' knaves";

and the Highlands are doubly driven:

> "An' Highlandmen hate tolls and taxes."

Tolls and taxes are an acquired taste, and the Highlands, lately brought in, like the territories lately annexed to Glasgow, do not yet appreciate their privileges.

Some details of the fiscal distress appear. Old imposts are revised:

> "And cesses, stents, and fees are raxed";

fresh ones are devised, and labourers over their beer

> "tell what new taxation's coming."

Burns himself suggests "some scheme like tea or winnocks." But he strongly objects to a proposed tax on riding horses:

> "Thro' dirt and dub for life I'll paiddle,
> Ere I sae dear pay for a saddle;
> Sae dinna put me in your buke,
> Nor for my ten white shillings luke";

and, little thinking he is himself to be a gauger, he flames out against

> "Thae curst horse-leeches o' th' excise
> Wha mak' the whisky stells their prize."

In one direction only, like many of ourselves, he protests against economy: taxes or no taxes, he cries to King George,

> "For God's sake! let nae saving fit
> Abridge your bonny barges
> An' boats this day!"

XVIII.

CURRENCY.

WE can construct from Burns's poems a complete set of the old Scotch coinage.

1. *The Boddle*, $\frac{1}{6}$ of a 1d. sterling:

"Fair play, he caredna deils a boddle."

The lowest coin of a currency is sometimes taken as the measure of the wealth of a people. On this principle we are six times richer than we used to be. The farthing is obsolete, and it is only thanks to halfpenny newspapers and halfpenny tram fares, that the halfpenny survives.

2. *The Plack*, $\frac{1}{3}$ of 1d. sterling:

"In my last plack thy parts be in't,
The better half o't!"

Not a large patrimony after all for Burns's "dear-bought Bess," especially as there were other claimants to the fund *in medio*. *Legitimatio per subsequens matrimonium* would have been more to the purpose. No doubt it would have cost Burns more than many placks; but it would have lifted his "sweet wee Betty" out of the low estate of bastardy, and, would have made an honest woman of a mother not wanting in "person, grace, and merit."

3. *The Bawbee*, ½d. sterling:

"I'll gi'e John Ross anither bawbee
To boat me o'er to Charlie."

4. *The Groat*, 4d. sterling:

"He will win a shilling
Or he spend a groat."

5. *The Tester*, 6d. sterling:

"Your sair taxation does her fleece
Till she has scarce a tester."

6. *The Mark*, 13⅓d. sterling:

"He gied me thee, o' tocher clear,
An' fifty mark:
Tho' it was sma', 'twas weel-won gear,
An' thou was stark."

The mark was $\frac{2}{3}$ of £1 Scots, *i.e.* of 20d. sterling. It is multiples of this coin that give the curious odd amounts found in the interval between the appearance of the £1 sterling and the disappearance of the £1 Scots, *e.g.* £5 11s. 1$\frac{1}{3}$d. = 100 Marks, £27 15s. 6$\frac{2}{3}$d. = 500 Marks. What the auld farmer got from his guid-father was £2 15s. 6$\frac{2}{3}$d. = 50 Marks, along with the immortal Maggie.

7. *The Guinea*, £1 1s. sterling:

> "To proper young men he'll clink in the hand
> Gowd guineas a hunder or twa, man."

> "The rank is but the guinea stamp."

Fifty years ago, before the invasion of English tourists and English sportsmen, we never saw a gold coin outside of a museum, and we looked askance at the now ever welcome sovereign. Our native bank-paper, especially the ancient trusty 'Pun Not,' was the universal currency. It was not so in Burns's day. He never once names bank notes. Gold— gold guineas, not sovereigns—is his regular currency above the mark. It's the lad's want of "the yellow dirt" that makes Tibbie "cast her head anither airt"; it is "gowd" that auld Rob Morris has in his coffers; it is the "yellow-lettered Geordies" that keek through the steeks of the Laird's purse; it is a "yellow George," a "gowd guinea" that Burns is fined in "the Poacher Court"; it is the "sweet yellow darlings wi' Geordie imprest," the "nice yellow guineas" that attract the fortune-hunter. The guinea is indicated even when not named,

"That one pound one I sairly want it";

and if large sums are given in pounds, the idea of the metal is still there:

"Ten thousand glittering pounds a year."

XIX.

PRICES.

A FEW prices come up incidentally.

"Twal penny worth o' nappy,"

i.e. 1d. worth sterling, is a treat "whyles" to be had by a party of labourers. The "cutty sark o' Paisley harn"—most famous of sarks, more famous than the *chemise de la Reine Isabelle*—costs "twa pund Scots," or 3s. 4d. sterling, which is "a' the riches" of a decent old woman. Lining costs a shade under 4d. a yard:

"When ilka ell cost me a groat,
 The Taylor staw the linin' o't."

The Mossgiel cowt, "o' cowts the wale," the

breeder expects to

> ". . . draw him fifteen pun' at least."

There have been actual sales of six of dear auld Maggie's progeny

> "at thretteen punds an' twa,
> The vera warst."

If "tippeny" has ceased to be a sure guide to the price of the liquor with which "we fear nae evil," "tippence" is what "we maun draw" for the plate at the Kirkgate. Threepence is airles for a fee'd man:

> "I fee'd a man at Martinmas
> Wi' airle pennies three."

No doubt the fee was in proportion to the modest airles. A woman's wage would be still less: the Collier Laddie's Lass probably exaggerates when she boasts

> "I can win my five pennies in a day";

Burns himself declares

> "On eighteenpence a-week I've lived before."[1]

---

[1] In the parish of Ayr in 1791 a farm-hand with some little help from his wife could earn 7s. a week, "some-

These figures, low as they sound to us, are not conclusive as to the condition of the people. Figures are uncertain guides in economics; wages may be swelled by "guid fat braxies" and other perquisites; rents by coals, kain, and other stents; and money varies indefinitely in purchasing power. But they were undeniably poor, very poor, in the Land of Burns.

"An auld clay biggan," with "ragged roof and chinky wall," is the house of a farmer in a pretty big way; braxy mutton, *i.e.* fa'en meat, is a luxury; a New-Year party have only one "luntin pipe" among them, and smoke in turns; the "nits" have been "weel hoarded" for the Hallowe'en festivities;

---

times a little more." See Sinclair's *Statistical Account*, article by Drs. Dalrymple and M'Gill. A *resident* farm-hand (board reckoned at £5) had £7 in money. This was what Burns and his brother Gilbert, both of them good hands, had from their father when they lived with him and worked to him. Out of the £7 the old man stopped the value of any home-made clothes the young men got.

"a pickle nits" (graphic phrase) "and twa red cheekit apples" outweigh Sawney's fears to "meet the Deil"; tenant-bodies are "faughten and harassed" to make ends meet; and cot folk are constantly "on poortith's brink":

> "An' when they meet wi' sair disasters,
> Like loss o' health, or want o' maisters,
> Ye maist wad think a wee touch langer
> An' they maun starve o' cauld an' hunger."

The general distress can be traced to a decay in the good old ways:

> "Nae langer thrifty citizens, an' douce,
> Meet owre a pint, or in the Council-house;
> Yet staumrel, corky-headed, graceless gentry,
> The herryment an' ruin o' the country."

And decadence is not confined to economics. Even the speech has degenerated. In the good old days

"They spak' their thoughts in plain braid lallans":

now the very pulpit is affected:

> "Nae langer, Rev'rend Men, their country's glory,
> In plain braid Scots hold forth a plain braid story."

Alas for that Golden Age that always, always, is past and gone!

XX.

RECREATIONS.

THE Scotch, though a serious, have never been a dull people, and Burns's contemporaries had their recreations, high or low.

OF THE GENTRY.

Some amusements of the gentry that he names are still in vogue:

1. *Hunting:*

    "Our whipper-in, wee blastit wonner";

    "An' thro' the whins, an' by the cairn
    Whare hunters fand the murdered bairn."

2. *Shooting:*

    "Now wastlin' wind and slaughtrin' guns
    Bring autumn pleasant weather";

[handwritten margin note: Commenta on the trival things the rich took part in]

"The hunter now has left the moor,
The scattered coveys meet secure."

3. *Fishing:*

"At noon the fisher seeks the glen";

"The trout within yon wimplin' burn
Glides swift, a silver dart,
An' safe beneath the shady thorn,
Defies the angler's art."

Sport in those days was not beyond the reach of men of modest means. Tam Samson, the Kilmarnock seedsman, can command a mixed shooting of "mawkins," and "birring paitricks," and "cootie moorcocks," where

"pointers round impatient burn'd,
Frae couples freed,"

and a fishing where

"the stately saumont sail,
And trout be-dropp'd wi' crimson hail,
And eels weel kent for souple tail,
And geds for greed."

Our friend the poacher is in full force. Death has no doubt borrowed his "three-tae'd leister" from the illicit hunter of the "stately sawmont," and the resident laird, who

"Ne'er a bit is hard on puir folk,"

RECREATIONS

has no mercy on the lawless "shootin' o' a hare or moorcock."

The gentry relieve the horrible tedium by wilder excitements than sport:

> "But Gentlemen, an' Ladies warst,
> Wi' ev'n-down want o' wark are curst.
> . . . .
> The men cast out in party matches,
> Then sowther a' in deep debauches;
> Ae nicht they're mad wi' drink an' whoring,
> Neist day their life is past enduring."

The ladies:

> "lee-lang nichts, wi' crabbit leuks,
> Pore ower the devil's pictur'd beuks;
> Stake on a chance a farmer's stack-yard,
> An' cheat like ony unhang'd blackguard."

These ploys speaking broadly are now as obsolete as flintlocks or samplers, but I could not say that the men have given up their

> "balls and races,
> Their galloping thro' public places,"

or that the leddies never

> "O'er the wee bit cup and platie,
> Sip the scandal potion pretty";

only, they do it now over the afternoon tea,

not in the weary after-dinner wait till the men should stagger into the drawing-room.

There are repeated allusions to Freemasonry: "honours masonic," "the masons' mystic word an' grip," "brothers of the mystic tie," "the brethren of the mystic level," "wi' jads or masons," Burns in these reflecting rather his own habits than the habits of his class.

OF THE COMMON FOLK.

The poor have their recreations too, much needed and much enjoyed, for when

> "fatigued wi' close employment,
> A blink o' rest's a sweet enjoyment!"

HOLIDAYS.

Holidays dot the year.

1. *New Year's Day:*

"That merry day the year begins."

2. *Yule* (old style, not 25th December, but 5th January):

"On blithe yule nicht when we were fou."

3. *Valentine's Day*:

> "Yestreen at the valentine's dealing
> My heart to my mou' gied a sten."

4. *Shrove Tuesday*:

> "On Fasten-e'en we had a rockin."

5. *All Saints Eve*: when

> "merry friendly kintra folks
> Together did convene,
> To burn their nits, an' pou their stocks,
> And haud their Hallowe'en."

6. *All Saints Day*:

> "As bleakfac'd Hallowmass returns [1]
> They get the jovial ranting kirns."

FUNCTIONS.

1. *Weddings*:

> "At kirns and weddings we'se be there,"

is part of the fiddler's proffer to the "raucle carlin."

A special feature of weddings was the

---

[1] Perhaps "Hallowmass" is only another way of saying Hallowe'en.

Broose.[1] The auld farmer tells his auld Mare Maggie,

> "At Brooses thou had ne'er a fellow
>   For pith and speed."

2. *Rockins*, gatherings at which the girls spin, or are supposed to spin, with rock and spindle.

> "At Fasten-e'en we had a rockin,
>   To ca' the crack and weave our stockin',
>   An' there was muckle fun and jokin',
>   Ye needna doubt."

---

[1] The Broose was a very ancient marriage custom, now, I fear, extinct. The young cavaliers of the party, as soon as they had kissed her after the marriage, mounted at the door of the bride's house and raced to the bridegroom's, the winner having the privilege to receive the bride at her new home. There, like her Roman sister, she was lifted over the threshold, lest she should make an unlucky stumble, and, once inside the door, she had a farl of oat-cake or shortbread broken over her head, in sign that she should never want. The cavaliers galloped off to a very old tune, "She's yours, she's yours, she's nae mair oors," better known as "John Paterson's Mare," the tune sung to "The Battle o' Sherriffmuir." Brooses were run in the Monklands within our own time: "Sandy Baird" of Gartsherrie was a noted brooser in his younger days.

3. *The Kirn* or *Harvest Home*, a notable function—"the rattlin' Kirn," "the rantin' Kirn," "the rantin' jovial Kirn," "that merry nicht we get the corn in." In those days of backward husbandry, the Kirn has a chance to coincide with Hallowe'en:

> "The simmer had been cauld an' wat,
> An' stuff was unco green,
> An' aye a rantin' kirn we gat,
> An' jist on Hallowe'en
> It fell that nicht."

4. *Races.* It is at

> "Mauchline race or Mauchline fair"

that Burns gives Lapraik his choice as rendezvous.

5. *Markets, Fairs, and Trysts* are used for pleasure as well as profit:

> "That frae November till October,
> Ae market-day thou was nae sober";

> "For mony a plack they wheedle frae me
> At dance or fair."

It is at "the Tryste o' Dalgarnock" that the braw wooer meets his fate.

DANCING

is practised indoors and out:

> "Yestreen when tae the tremblin' string
> The dance gaed thro' the lichtet ha'";

> "He gaed wi' Jeanie to the tryste,
> An' danced wi' Jeanie on the down."

There is enough of it for the relative merits of performers to be weighed:

> "But when will he dance like Tam Glen?"

The dances in vogue are

> "Nae cotillon brent new frae France,"

but of a lively sort,

> "Hornpipes, jigs, strathspeys, and reels
> Put life and mettle in their heels";

> "There's threesome reels and foursome reels,
> There's hornpipes and strathspeys, man!"

MUSIC.

Music bulks largely among the pleasures of life. Burns himself had a fine taste in music: how could he else, the greatest of song writers? But music is never far to seek:

> "On Fasten-e'en . . .
> . . . we had a hearty yokin'
> At sang about";

on Hallowe'en

> "Wi' merry sangs and friendly cracks,
> I wat they dinna weary";

Tam o' Shanter forgets the rough road home, and the rough welcome that waits him, as

> "The night drave on wi' sangs an' clatter";

at Poosie Nansie's splore

> "They ranted and they sang";

and the singers have got beyond mere plain song, and

> "Round and round take up the chorus."

There is an ample *repertoire*. From his pack the "wight of Homer's craft"

> "wales a sang,
> A ballad o' the best";

and from

> "Those strains that once did sweet in Zion glide"

the " priest-like father "

" . . . wales a portion with judicious care."

We have the very melodies. At the Ordination, with a liberal allowance of "double verses four," they

" . . . skirl up the Bangor";

fechtin' Jamie Fleck "keeps his courage cheery" to the tune of Lord Lennox' March;

"An' Scotland draws her pipe and blaws,
 'Up, Willie, war them a', man!'"

to meet their "impatience for the chorus," the "jovial throng" at Poosie Nansie's have "Jolly Mortals, fill your glasses"; and to "beet the heavenward flame,"

"Perhaps Dundee's wild warbling measures rise,
Or plaintive Martyrs, worthy of the name;
Or noble Elgin . . .
The sweetest far of Scotia's holy lays."

The taste for song is of old standing. Tam o' Shanter "skelps through dub and mire,"

"Whiles crooning o'er some auld Scotch sonnet,"

and sorrow and care are to be cured

"Wi' a cog o' guid swats an' an auld Scottish song."

The taste is not even confined to Scottish song. The owner of Luath has named that "gash an' faithfu' tyke" "after some dog in Highland song."

There are many song-makers in the Land of Burns besides "rhyming Robin, *alias* Burns." At Ochiltree is "winsome Willie" Simpson; at Tarbolton Davie Sillar, "ace o' hearts; at Muirkirk "bauld Lapraik, the king o' hearts"; at Adamhill "rough, rude, ready-witted Rankine."

And the very process is detailed by which they evolve their songs from the old music:

> "On braes when we please, then,
> We'll sit an' sowth a tune;
> Syne rhyme till't, we'll time till't,
> And sing't when we ha'e done."

How easy it all is, to be sure!

We have instrumental music as well as vocal. There is not the variety of it that might at first seem. I don't believe that the shepherd in the "birken shaw" really "stopp'd his simple reed," or that the old bard who laments Glencairn actually had a "trembling harp." I am not even sure, in spite of all the "chanters" named, that there was any literal piper in the Land of Burns, except the "towsie tyke" who made the "roof and rafters dirl" in Kirk Alloway. But there is no mistake about the fiddlers; they are real flesh and blood—"little Sir Violino," "the fairy fiddler," "the poor gut-scraper,"

> "The pigmy scraper wi' his fiddle,
> Wha used at trysts and fairs to driddle,"

is evidently a portrait, and "M'Lauchlan, thairm-inspiring sage" is the rival of the great Neil Gow.

The fiddle leads the dance:

> "Yestreen, when tae the tremblin' string
> The dance gaed through the lichted ha'!"

it is a resource in trouble:

> "Hale be your heart! Hale be your fiddle;
> Lang may your elbuck jink and diddle,
> Tae cheer you thro' the weary widdle
>   O' war'ly cares";

and the fiddler loves his instrument as the Arab loves his horse:

> "An' parting wi' his fiddle,
> The saut tear blin't his e'e."

GAMES.

1. *Football:*

   > "However fortune kick the ba'";
   > "Pursuing fortune's sliddery ba'."

2. *Curling:*

   > "When to the lochs the curlers flock
   > Wi' gleesome speed";
   > "The curlers quat their roarin' play."

3. *Golfing:*

   > "But, word an' blow, North, Fox, and Co.
   > Gowffed Willie like a ba', man."

Cricket of course is not named, nor, curiously enough, shinty.

There is no notice of bathing. Swimming is once mentioned, but rather as a dire alternative:

> "There's men o' taste wad tak the Ducat stream,
> Tho' they should cast the very sark and swim."

"Fechtin'" Jamie Fleck was a devotee of the oldest and simplest of all sports.

TOBACCO.

The virtues of the soothing weed had been discovered in the Land of Burns. Tobacco is both snuff'd and smoked:

> "The luntin' pipe and sneeshin' mull
> Are handed round wi' richt guid will."

Ladies sometimes smoke, as they sometimes, 'tis whispered, do in our own days. At wee Jenny's impious daring, Grannie

> "fuff'd her pipe wi' sic a lunt,
> In wrath she was sae vap'rin',
> She noticed na, an aizle brunt
> Her braw new worset apron
> Out thro' that night."

The pleasures of strong drink are referred to on pages 55-59.

The pleasures of one other appetite and their vogue come up over and over and over again in Burns: lust runs liquor hard. If the picture he draws of the profligacy of his day is the truth, or anything like the truth, we may be thankful that we live in times when profligacy is less rampant, and profligates are less shameless. No Juvenal of our day would paint a country magnate as using his power to punish "for speaking lichtly of his limmer," or "Racer Jess and twa three whores" as "blinking at the entry" of a church bazaar; no libertine of our day would write to a man he had never seen, an old man of sixty, as Burns at twenty-six writes to Lapraik, of his *bonnes fortunes* with poor country girls, or would put his hand to the "Address to an Illegitimate Daughter."

One remark and I have done. It will be long before the stream run dry of pilgrims to the scenes that Burns has sung into fame;

but the number of the pilgrims who understand, or at least appreciate, his poems, who catch the full flavour of the nectar, lessens year by year. People have lately founded a Chair of Gaelic. They had better have founded a Chair of Scotch. Gaelic, with its scientific structure and its relations to other languages, will always interest a handful of philologists, but its popular influence will be *nil*, or will be hurtful: there is no literature to reward the laborious study, and he is no friend to the Highlands who would do anything tending to keep apart Celt and Saxon. A study of Scotch would have the opposite effect. One of the strongest ties that used here to bind class to class was a common literature. Gentle and semple alike were familiar with at least two books, their Bible and their Burns. I will not ask how strong the common interest still is in the Bible, but Burns is grown almost a dead language to the quality, and even the common folk, thanks to School Boards and other modern influences, are fast losing their good Scotch. A return to the old conditions would at least be a make-weight (and we have none too many of the sort) in drawing us together: "sympathy is the universal solvent." And Scotch is well worth studying for its own sake. It is easy, and it is interesting; it was the speech, high and low, of an eager, a humorous, an imaginative race, and has come down from them the purest, the tersest, the most graphic form of English, and if it had no literature in it but Burns, one song of his has as much poetry in it, as much passion and pathos, as—dare I say it?—all Ossian.

THE END.

GLASGOW: PRINTED AT THE UNIVERSITY PRESS
BY ROBERT MACLEHOSE AND CO.

www.ingramcontent.com/pod-product-compliance
Lightning Source LLC
Chambersburg PA
CBHW030343170426
43202CB00010B/1225